Simply
Scandinavian

Simply Scandinavian

CONTRIBUTING EDITOR Sara Norrman

WITH ADDITIONAL TEXT BY **MAGNUS ENGLUND**
AND **CAROLINE CLIFTON-MOGG**

RYLAND PETERS & SMALL
LONDON • NEW YORK

Senior designer Megan Smith
Editor Delphine Lawrance
Picture research Emily Westlake
Head of production Patricia Harrington
Art director Leslie Harrington
Publishing director Alison Starling

First published in 2010.
This updated edition published in 2016
by Ryland Peters and Small
20–21 Jockey's Fields
London WC1R 4BW
and
Ryland Peters & Small, Inc.
341 E 116th Street
New York, NY 10029
www.rylandpeters.com

10 9 8 7 6 5 4 3

Text © Ryland Peters & Small,
Caroline Clifton-Mogg, Jo Denbury
and Magnus Englund 2010, 2016
Design and photographs
© Ryland Peters & Small 2010, 2016
See pages 156-157 for further credits.

ISBN: 978-1-84975-729-4

Library of Congress Cataloging-in-
Publication Data for the original edition of
this book is as follows:

Simply Scandinavian / contributing
editor, Sara Norrman.
    p. cm.
  Includes index.
  ISBN 978-1-84597-977-5
  1. Interior decoration--Scandinavia--
Themes, motives. I. Norrman, Sara.
  NK2057.S56 2010
  747--dc22
                    2009048373

contents

introduction

Interior trends come and go, but Scandinavian style remains. Homes in the Nordic countries – Sweden, Finland, Norway, Denmark and Iceland – have a relaxed way of living that is copied and emulated the world over. These countries are incredibly varied in cultural heritage, but all share a very similar design aesthetic – from Tromsø to Esbjerg, Scandinavian homes are light, friendly and simply gorgeous.

In this book, we showcase a range of stylish homes, from Ilkka Suppanen's minimalist dream home on an island off the Finnish coast, to Anja Alfieri's feminine and ornate house in southern Sweden. They are miles apart when it comes to aesthetics, but are both unmistakably Scandinavian – there is an illusive quality that unites them. This quality could be the unique light on these northern shores that gives any interior a dream-like and slightly melancholy aspect. Or perhaps it is simply the owners' eternal quest for said light – in countries that see whole months of near-total darkness, the need to create homes that invite in the smallest of sunrays is overwhelming.

Households in Scandinavia did away with dark furniture and heavy textiles on a larger scale from as early as the mid-1950s. The post-war era brought with it a revolution in design and architecture that went hand in hand with the social democratic political movement that swept the nations – good design,

like free healthcare and schooling, was available to everybody. As opposed to many other movements, the Scandinavian look has not grown out of palaces, unlike the gilded splendour of French baroque, nor from the imports of exotic colonies, as in the swathed shapes of Victorian Britain. Scandinavian style is affordable, practical yet beautiful — it is a form of design that works hard on all levels.

A love of pale and muted colours can be seen in most homes. You can decorate with any colour in a Scandinavian interior — as long as it's white. And the white palette runs the whole gamut from the brightest gallery whites to the softly pale grey Gustavian whites — it is, perhaps, the interiors equivalent to the many words for snow in the Inuit language.

But if the walls, floors and ceilings remain stubbornly quiet, there has always been scope for loud and colourful textiles and accessories in Nordic homes. In the Swedish county of Dalarna, the 18th-century kurbits paintings on cupboards and chests are flamboyantly bright, while Finnish traditional clothing comes embroidered with roses that are far from pared back. This love of joyful textiles continues to this day, with the larger-than-life blooms of Marimekko.

When it comes to designers worth name-droppping, Scandinavia is second perhaps only to Italy. This mix between cutting-edge designs and more traditional craft is a winning combination in Scandinavian design — revolutionary items like the Cobra phone, Verner Panton's moulded plastic chair and the PH light now exist

happily alongside a thriving craft-based industry, with Nordic linen, glass and ironwork enjoying a revival.

The main inspiration in Nordic homes is taken from right outside the window – nature. The Scandinavians were bringing the outside in, in the shape of wooden floors and wool rugs, when everybody else in Europe was busy laying synthetic carpets. Even highly designed items take natural shapes, like Alvar Aalto's iconic Savoy vase, which is shaped like an undulating beach line.

Wood is perhaps the most common of the natural materials, due of course to the abundance of forests. Other popular materials that are an instant Scandi hit in the home are stone, hides, felt and pewter – when it comes to metal, bling is bad; think brass instead of gold, or pewter instead of silver. The open flame is also an important component – many homes have wood-fired ovens. Modern households that have only central heating are still fond of lighting candles, to create a cozy ambience.

As much as Scandinavians love their homes, they are also (and have always been) avid travellers. Many interiors bear traces of journeys abroad, and treasures brought back from exotic lands often sit comfortably with the calm Nordic interiors. Mixing local and foreign is one Scandinavian knack; mixing old and new is another. This is partly due to environmental awareness and partly a pride in heritage and traditions. Whatever the history, natural backdrop or design heritage, when styles are mixed up, it creates homes that are all about relaxed comfort; places where everybody should feel at home. And perhaps this is the elusive component that defines Scandinavian homes – it's a style that is so much more than fabric swatches or paint samples. It's a style formed by life.

Elegant Simplicity

One of the clearest examples of Scandinavian elegance comes in the form of the Gustavian style, which was inspired by the French court in the late 18th century. But on their way north, the lines of the adorned chairs and cabinets became simpler, the colours toned down and the luxurious fabrics substituted for tougher materials – all the better to suit the simpler conditions and harsher usage in the homes of Scandinavia where the furniture ended up taking residence. Today, Gustavian furniture with its elegantly simple lines in pale greys and whites remains popular. The timeless look has been updated and reproduced many a time since, and sits equally well in a modern house as in a manor.

norwegian wood

Brekkestø is a small village located on the southern coast of Norway, in a region known as Sørlandet (the South Land). The village forms part of the municipality of Lillesand, in the county of Aust-Agder. These might all sound like geographical references lifted directly from *The Lord of the Rings*, and indeed could well be, given that J. R. R. Tolkien was an expert on Scandinavian languages, in particular old Norwegian and Icelandic.

Fishing and sailing are still important industries in Norway, and its coast is made up of long fjords, cutting deep into the country. The history of Brekkestø is closely connected with these activities. During winter, when the fjords freeze over, the seafarers of old had to base their fleets as far out into the ice-free ocean as possible so that they would be in a position to set sail early each spring. Villages

ABOVE The extension table in Gustavian style in the dining room is early 20th century. It may well be made up of several unrelated parts that have been put together. **RIGHT** When the tide is high, the water line reaches right up to the front of the house. The water retreats after a few hours, its salt impregnating the timber and making it rock hard.

OPPOSITE The central core of the house is clad in raw timber that has been painted, while the rooms leading off it have plastered walls. The house seems to be full of pieces of furniture that have been there for years, but the reality is different; old fishing houses such as this one often relied on foreign imports.

OPPOSITE The bedroom is one of the few rooms in the house where the colour scheme has veered from white or cream tones. The large bed dates from the early 20th century and is the focal point, thanks to its vintage floral bedspread. **BELOW LEFT** Norwegian merchant vessels such as the one in this painting were already crossing the oceans in the early 18th century, just as they do today. Even the Antarctic was within their reach, as the Norwegian names given to many remote islands illustrate. The seating in front makes for a tranquil reading spot and matches the style of the light furniture dotted around the house, most of which is from Denmark or Norway. **BELOW CENTRE** The harbour bed outside the house holds artefacts derived from 400 years of maritime activity. It is not unusual to come across old bottles, chalk pipes, glass floats and other relics. Some of these objects have made their way into the house as eyecatching, unique decorations. **BELOW RIGHT** The house's location right by the sea is reflected in the owners' choice of items used to decorate it. This brass hook has a distinctive nautical style and sits perfectly on the timber-clad wall.

with harbours were located on the extremities of the coast, and Brekkestø is one of those villages. In summer, the ships would be out at sea and Brekkestø empty of menfolk, but in winter the village would become a veritable hive of activity. Ropemakers, carpenters, smiths and sailmakers repaired and re-equipped the ships in the harbour in preparation for the following spring. They all needed lodging, and the village inn was the establishment that provided it. The house featured in these pages was that same inn.

Brekkestø is spread over several rocky islands. The nearest town is Lillesand, accessible by a network of roads and bridges. Many of the homes built around Brekkestø's compact harbour are white wooden cottages with red-tiled roofs, typical of the area, giving the place a very quaint feel. Early 20th-century writers and painters such as Christian Krohg, Nils Kjær and Gabriel Scott retreated to Brekkestø in search of inspiration during the quiet summers. That said, nowadays the small village is often crowded with tourists during the peak summer months, while in winter the village is virtually deserted – precisely the opposite of the situation that prevailed 100 or even 50 years ago.

The old inn was built some time around 1750; no one knows the date or year exactly. The style is similar to the houses that were being built in New England at the same

LEFT The seamen of a century or more ago frequently brought back with them furniture found during their travels abroad. This house is full of old pieces, mostly from Norway or Denmark, in the 18th-century Gustavian style, which remains a popular choice in Scandinavia.

OPPOSITE The sofa by the window is Danish and from the 18th century. The ship model on the wall, known as a half-model, was common in the mid-19th century. It holds a miniature ship cut in half and then glued onto the bottom of the box. The chest of drawers beneath is also Danish, possibly dating from the late 17th century.

time. The inn is right next to the water, built on an old seabed that has been reclaimed by filling it with rocks and stones. This may have been done in order to acquire the land cheaply, or to avoid having to seek building permission, but no one knows for sure. What is a certainty is that the house is so close to the water that, when the owners open a hatch in the floor, they can see crabs crawling underneath. When the tide is high – and it does get very high every other year or so – the water reaches right up to the front door of the house. For a new house made from modern building materials,

this would spell disaster, but in this case it doesn't seem to bother it – the water retreats after a few hours anyway.

The present occupiers have owned the house for some 50 years, and were among the first summer visitors to buy a house in Brekkestø rather than choosing to lodge with the village's permanent inhabitants. When you enter the house, it appears to be filled with pieces of furniture that have been there since the house was built, but the reality is quite different. The seamen of 100 or 200 years ago often brought their furniture from abroad, from Victorian Britain or

The inn is right next to the water, built on an old sea bed that has been reclaimed.

Imperial Germany. The style of that time was dark and heavy, far from the type of furniture featured today. The current furniture is also old, but most of it comes from Norway or Denmark and is in a much lighter style. The sandy shore outside the house is a repository of artefacts that bear witness to 400 years of activity, some of which have made their way into the house as decorative objects. Another reminder of the working life at sea are the flags from Norwegian merchant vessels.

The present owners are keen sailors and keep several boats. They generally use the house from April until October. Autumn is usually cold and windy, but it is also the start of the lobster-fishing season – a good incentive to stay behind. People travel to Brekkestø from far and wide to buy fresh fish or try their own luck at fishing.

ABOVE The old inn was built some time around 1750, right by the water, on a reclaimed seabed. The present owners are keen sailors and they keep several boats. There are also boats available for making deep-sea fishing expeditions further out in the Atlantic Ocean. The house is so close that a hatch in the floor opens to reveal crabs crawling about beneath it. OPPOSITE The flags from Norwegian merchant vessels used to decorate the entrance to the house are a reminder of the long tradition of maritime activity in Brekkestø. The staircase is as steep as that on any ship. The bottom of it is decorated with a dolphin, a species that is found in the seas nearby.

family friendly

ABOVE Among the most useful of all kitchen furniture items is the multi-functional island unit. **ABOVE RIGHT** This dining area is firmly in the Scandinavian style, with its blend of old and new furniture, antiques and contemporary design classics, teamed with decorative silver and glass. All is designed to make the most of the short winter days, where daylight is at a premium.

There are as many different ways to arrange an apartment as there are ways to live in one. One route is to make major structural and decorative changes and to reconfigure the space totally. Another is to go along with what already exists and change your way of life to suit the space. A third, and perhaps the most practical option, is to make a few changes and, with those as your starting point, concentrate on the important personal details that will make the space your own, and that will suit every family member.

Kamilla Byriel and Christian Permin have taken the latter, more pragmatic route. Their apartment in Copenhagen is light, bright and peaceful, making it hard to believe that it is home not only to Kamilla and Christian but also to their three small children. Under different circumstances, it might be a mess; amazingly, it is calm and well ordered. That is not because

THIS PAGE In the central living room is a pair of wicker PK 22 chairs by Poul Kjærholm, defined by another wicker piece that looks like an oversized bottle gourd. Beneath the window is a workman's bench used as a table, with an arrangement of candlesticks and flowers in decorative juxtaposition.

THIS PAGE The view along the length of the apartment from the far room into the kitchen shows that space flow need not be hard to arrange. Here, merely closing off the door from the hall turned this into a comfortable room, as well as an area that leads the eye easily from one end to the other.

Kamilla and Christian run a particularly tight ship; it is simply that they have thought logically about the space available and have decided to take what is there and make it work for them in the most comfortable way they can. Kamilla is part of an innovative clothing company, Stella Nova, which might well explain her design and organizational abilities.

One of the first, and possibly simplest, decisions Kamilla and Christian made was that family life would take place on the upper floor of the apartment, with each of the children's bedrooms becoming a combination of playroom and bedroom. It is cheerful and messy up there, but the arrangement works because it means that downstairs is relatively free of clutter, calm and friendly. It's not a child-free zone by any means, for the children are most welcome downstairs and spend most of their time there; rather, all the paraphernalia of childhood is kept not only out of sight but also in a place of its own.

The living floor consists of two rooms that run into each other, with a kitchen at one end that extends across the whole width of the house. When Kamilla and Christian moved in, the middle room, instead of being a living space, was a wide hall that led to the kitchen in one direction and the small living room in the other. They closed up the doors into the hall from the corridor, creating a large extra living space that linked one end of the apartment with the other. The middle room is now a family room complete with a sofa that is large enough to seat the whole family at once – perfect for convivial film viewings.

The long kitchen is the hub of the apartment, even outside of mealtimes. At one end, a wide window provides light for the old wooden work table, which is now used as a dining table; at the other end, there is an all-white kitchen area with an island unit, containing the hob along with

ABOVE The kitchen is the heart of this home. Everywhere there are small decorative touches, such as this table with two posters on and above it, as well as pieces of china and glass. **RIGHT** This 1950s Swan chair by Arne Jacobsen complements the clean lines of the apartment.

storage for pots and pans, and a sink unit against the wall. As in the rest of the apartment, the floors have been painted high-shine white, as have the ceilings and walls. Scandinavian winters can be long and the days short, so there is an instinctive desire among the population to catch as much of the fleeting light as possible.

Since Kamilla and Christian had decided against major structural work, they knew that it was the details that would make the apartment theirs – in particular, the carefully chosen furniture and the placing of objects. The couple are proud of their Scandinavian design heritage, and the furniture in the apartment ranges from 19th-century family pieces to iconic, recognizable items from the 20th century. In the kitchen, for example, is an antique, glass-fronted cupboard inherited by Kamilla, and lights by Verner Panton, while in the far sitting room is the open leaf-shaped, black leather Swan chair designed by Arne Jacobsen. 'You can use his pieces anywhere in a house,' says Kamilla. 'If you have a few basic pieces, they can go with you through your life, and each piece of furniture here has its own story, something which is very important to us.' The way it is combined is also important. As Kamilla says, 'It's all to do with the mix,' which means combining the modern and the antique in clever and unusual ways.

There are no curtains in the apartment, nor, except in the middle room, are there any rugs. It might be thought that this lack of furnishings would make the space rather cold, but, on the contrary, it is as warm and welcoming as if it were hung with textiles from ceiling to floor. This is the effect Kamilla wanted to achieve, for as she says, 'The weather here is not very nice and we spend a lot of time indoors, so it's important to us to have somewhere that is comfortable, functional and personal too.'

ABOVE This dining area is firmly in the Scandinavian country style, with its blend of old and new furniture, antiques and mid-20th-century design classics, combined with decorative silver and glass. The pale-coloured walls and curtainless windows are deliberate. All is designed to make the most of the short winter days in the north, where daylight is in short supply and must be capitalized on whenever possible.

THIS PAGE The antique wooden work table that is used as a dining table can seat at least eight and is set with an ever-changing selection of chairs, some vintage wooden ones, some made from moulded fibreglass by Charles and Ray Eames.

GEORGES BRAQUE

GALERIE MAEGHT

natural purity

This house is a real family affair. Not only does it play home to jewellery designer Charlotte Lynggaard, her husband Michel, four kids and a dog but it is designed to be as welcoming as possible for guests — of which there are many.

The rooms are spacious and airy, centring around the massive kitchen where the family spends most of its time. The outdoor areas, around the garden and terraces, are also dedicated to spending time together eating, drinking, playing and enjoying the stunning views over the sea.

In the living room, a big open fire is perfect for warming up after having taken a snowy walk in winter, and there is another massive grate in the kitchen where there is space for all the kids to roast apples or marshmallows.

The open-plan kitchen has a towering ceiling with beams running across it, and two

ABOVE The views over the bright blue sea in summer make the decking area an unbeatable spot for alfresco entertaining. A white umbrella and the tall fir trees provide just enough shade. **ABOVE RIGHT** Outside the rooms along the first floor runs a balcony that also faces the sea — perfect for that breath of fresh air first thing in the morning.

THIS PAGE The open fire takes pride of place in the living room and is a great source of heat in the cold winter months. A woven basket is perfect for holding logs and kindling. The rustic terracotta pot with its mini fig tree stands out against the strictly geometric coffee table.

ABOVE The high ceilings give the kitchen an almost church-like effect, and the grand space allows many people to be fed – it's easy to imagine convivial evenings here with a roaring fire and plenty of friends lined up around the table seated on classic Wishbone chairs by Hans J. Wegner. The stainless-steel kitchen units reflect the light from the tall doors opposite. **LEFT** The metal wire holder above the table holds photographs of the four children in the house. Vintage touches like a silver sugar bowl and pink rose stop the space looking too sparse.

skylights letting in the sun's rays high up on the walls – it almost feels like being in a long house, the traditional dwellings of the Vikings.

And despite its pale floors and white walls, Charlotte doesn't think that the kitchen ever feels cold or clinical, not even in winter. 'No, not at all! And especially not when the fire is blazing and we're making pancakes for everybody,' she says.

Charlotte is the daughter of legendary Danish jewellery designer Ole Lynggaard, and the two of them work side by side. Their designs can be found in exclusive boutiques all around the world, and they have become household names in Scandinavia. Like the house, the company is also focussed around family, as Charlotte's husband Michel is commercial director and her brother the CEO.

But the house was not always as welcoming as it is now. Built in 1926, when Charlotte found it, it was 'a romantic dream, but impossible to live in,' as she puts it. After an almost complete

ABOVE LEFT A good book in front of a warm radiator is always a treat. The painting is by the artist Raymond Moisset, and the floor lamp is a traditional Bestlite.

ABOVE Placing a large mirror on a wall that is out of direct sunlight opens up the space, and makes it feel much bigger. It also doubles the effect of the flowers.

ABOVE Textiles add a personal touch and a hint of colour to any home, no matter how unassuming their shade. The textures in this home are mainly traditional, from knitted blankets that are perfect for bundling up in and guarding oneself against the cold, to quilted throws and more masculine striped bedlinen and cushions. The beautiful beaded jewellery, again in muted tones, is made by Charlotte, who works with her famous father, Ole Lynggaard. Charlotte would love to design for leading ladies like Michelle Obama and Queen Rania of Jordan, and already has one royal follower – Mary, Crown Princess of Denmark is a fan.

overhaul, the north Copenhagen home now has 12 rooms with plenty of outdoor space and a variety of seating areas for the family to choose from.

The tall ceilings are complemented by the extra-wide blonde floorboards from Dinesen that run through the living areas of the house, and the floor-to-ceiling French doors let in as much light as possible.

Design classics like Hans J. Wegner's Wishbone chairs in the kitchen and Bestlite lamps create a timeless feel in the house, and keep it exciting visually.

This is a classically Scandinavian home, striving for light and filled with simple lines, but Charlotte is also inspired by Japan. This is seen clearly in the wet room, with its Zen-like calm, and also in her jewellery – it is delicate and feminine, but has an edge to it that surprises those who see it. 'I have travelled a lot in Japan, and brought home a lot of ideas and inspiration from the country,' Charlotte says.

In a house that is almost devoid of bright colours, textures take on a much bigger importance and also add warmth. The textiles in the house are pared-back and come in fairly traditional patterns – roughly knitted throws, delicately-flowered quilts and blue and white-striped bedlinen have been common in Danish homes for generations. These can be picked up easily in antiques stores and second-hand shops.

Texture is also important as a design component, from the glossy floorboards of the bedrooms, to the limestone tiles in the bathroom. These are more than just flooring options, playing a huge part in the total impact of the home – even the elements are involved, in the form of the flames in the grates and the water that stretches beyond the window. This is not a home that has been put together with colour charts and swatches, but with a gut feeling of what's right for the building itself and for the family that lives here.

THIS PAGE The cozy armchair is upholstered in an unusually strong pattern for this house, but it still reflects the colours of the deep-sea waters outside. The sheer curtains let through just enough light without blocking the view, and the glossy floorboards reflect the rays of the sun.

Design classics like Bestlite lamps create a timeless feel in the house, and keep it exciting visually.

THIS PAGE The wet room has an Asian feel, with the simple wooden stool and kimono-like bathrobe. The floor is made from limestone extracted from the quarries on the Swedish island of Öland, and looks extra good when wet. **OPPOSITE** The washbasin is wide enough for more than one person to brush their teeth in the morning, and the dark wood contrasts beautifully with the greenery outside, which is reflected in the large mirror.

LEFT A quiet corner in the shade is a good place to retreat to with a book and a glass of wine when the rest of the house gets a little too hectic.

But surely Charlotte must sometimes get an urge to paint a statement wall in a crazy pink, or to just introduce a bright blue cushion? 'No,' is the short and determined answer.

And seeing the house during the beautiful summer months, it's easy to understand Charlotte's reasons for this. The nature just outside the front door, teamed with the blue sky and wide sea, is stunning enough, without warranting any competition from brash decorating colours. The light in this part of the world has been celebrated by painters for

OPPOSITE The outdoor daybeds on this stretch of decking provide the perfect resting place on hot summer days, with magnificent views and Baltic breezes to cool the family down. The house enjoys a superb location where you are never too far away from a sea view, regardless of whether you are indoors or out. **BELOW (FROM LEFT TO RIGHT)** The humble cowslip takes on a beauty of its own set against the weather-beaten clapperboard. Small seashells and interesting stones have been turned into a thing of beauty by threading them on a string and letting them sway in the wind. The weathervane is in the shape of a fish — it might be able to show where the wind blows from, but whether it can point you in the direction of a fresh catch is another matter. White allium takes on a magical sheen when the blue dusk descends in summer.

decades, due to its blue hues that make summer nights melancholy in a very Scandinavian way.

The garden mirrors the simplicity of the house; it is filled with simple native blooms like lilacs, boxwood, hydrangea and roses, and there are plenty of wild flowers too — cow parsley takes on an unexpectedly delicate look when displayed in large bunches with tall stems.

This house was designed for a large family, which shows in the communal space that encourages socializing, but there are nooks and crannies for alone time too. A rattan chair on the terrace, with a basket of alliums placed next to it, is one of these peaceful spots; another is a single armchair in the living room, with a floor light above it making sure that solitary reading is possible.

And this is exactly how Charlotte and her family wanted their home to turn out when they moved in 13 years ago — their vision was for it to be somewhere to be together and sometimes apart; a cozy sanctuary yet a successful arena for the odd raucous party.

Or, as Charlotte says: 'The perfect home is where you can enjoy being with your family, go for walks, draw, paint, have parties, meditate — and dream…' Needless to say, the house and its beautiful environs have lived up to the family's expectations.

northern
lights

In Sweden, the days are brutally short through the cold months from mid-autumn to early spring, meaning that people have had to learn to value the soft beauty and healing effects of natural light.

The midpoint of the long, dark winter season – the longest night of the year – is marked by the Festival of Light, St Lucia's Day, in December, when celebrations centre around the lighting of many candles. Candlelight is an important feature at this converted distillery on a farm in southern Sweden. 'While we do have electric light, we rarely use it; instead we burn a large number of candles,' say the owners. 'Artificial light is so strong and cold, we prefer the warmth and glow – and the atmosphere of centuries long lost – that candlelight gives.'

The owners are mindful though of the destructive powers of naked flames and open fires. The distillery, being stone, is all that remains of the original period farm buildings that a fire destroyed just 30 years ago. The outbuildings have since been rebuilt in the Scandinavian softwood traditionally used as a building material.

OPPOSITE & ABOVE Gustavian style is both classical and minimalist. Furnishings are understated and sparsely arranged – a sense of space, freedom of movement and views between rooms are considered essential to creating an airy, light feel. Decoration comes in the form of elegant, light-enhancing accessories such as silver candlesticks and light ceramics. **LEFT** Everyday objects such as terracotta plant pots can be made to look like a beautiful still life when placed in the right setting; in this case a simple whitewashed background.

The farmstead is some distance from the nearest village, which gives it a romantic feeling of isolation that particularly appealed to the homeowners. 'For us there is a special feeling that comes from living in the country and being alone. The peace enhances our closeness to the elements, and we have the knowledge that nature is always just around the corner for us to enjoy.'

The owners are devotees of 18th- and 19th-century traditional Swedish style – Gustavian in particular – and are also antiques dealers. Their antiques shop is on the ground floor, while their living space on the first floor benefits from the extra light that being a little higher up affords.

The desire to exploit natural light is not a purely aesthetic one. Through the winter months, when the sun never rises above the surrounding treetops, spirits can be dimmed along with the sun's rays. The inhabitants of this hideaway recognize this fact and the corresponding need for a regular dose, quite literally, of sunlight to maintain health and

ABOVE LEFT Checks and stripes make perfect bedfellows in this otherwise simply decorated bedroom.

ABOVE CENTRE Pewter candlesticks are timeless and work well against the dark wooden tabletop.

ABOVE RIGHT The long dining table enjoys a prime location next to the window. Candlesticks are always to hand for when the nights draw in. The dark woods of the dresser and tabletop are offset perfectly by the light wooden chairs and white walls.

LEFT A bouquet of wild flowers in a jug makes a pleasing addition to any room.

BELOW & OPPOSITE In Scandinavia, softwood is commonly used for building and furniture, so over the years, paint finishes have been developed to protect it and to disguise its unsophisticated appearance. Rich warm colours like deep blue or red are used to merge buildings' exteriors with the landscape. The homeowners spend long periods of time during the lengthy summer days collecting firewood in the nearby forests, in preparation for the winter months when the fire takes centre stage in the farmstead, both for warmth and as an added source of natural light.

Heat-retaining small windows are offset by pale walls throughout the farmstead's interior.

happiness. Therefore, as is traditional in Swedish interiors, the layout of the converted distillery is designed and decorated with two conflicting aims in mind: being warm and cozy during the long winters while maximizing every last drop of precious daylight.

Heat-retaining small windows are offset by pale walls throughout the interior – painted with a traditional soft off-white distemper that reflects the light and complements the light-enhancing whites and grey-blues used on the painted furniture. Internal doors are 'glazed' with fine wire mesh to allow the hazy passage of light between rooms, and the windows have blinds, rather than obstructive curtains.

The owners' preference for firelight and candlelight as natural mood lighting immediately creates a warm ambience through the constantly flickering flames and shadows and the associated aromas of beeswax and pinewood that fill the house. The placing of mirrors, sconces and chandeliers combines with the soft light and magnifies it through reflection. It's an old device that originates in earlier centuries when candles were a luxury.

To fuel their passion for firelight, the owners spend the long daylight hours of summer collecting and chopping firewood in the surrounding forests, which they leave to dry ready for the harsh winter months.

simple style

When this beachside house was discovered by its present owners in 1998, it was a far cry from the comfortable young family home it has since become. The outside was covered in a plastic paint, the veranda fashioned out of shabby wood and the rooms were small and dark.

So the enthusiastic couple started by ripping out walls, stripping over-patterned wallpaper and changing the location of the kitchen.

The result is welcoming and cozy yet light and fresh. Culture and art take centre stage,

ABOVE Simple lines paired with a flower makes an impromptu still life and creates instant beauty on this distressed chair. **RIGHT** Books line the walls of this comfortable living room, while a model ship links the house to the nearby harbour. The cushions are a mix of Danish, Indian and French.

ABOVE The two sofas from Moroso have been placed purposefully to face each other. The framed artworks between the windows break up the big glassy expanse and also work brilliantly as a way to 'hide' the flatscreen television; without it as the centrepiece, the living room feels instantly more welcoming.

with plenty of books lining the walls of the living room, and numerous pictures and prints on display – some by well-established artists and others that will no doubt become well-known in the years to come.

The husband and wife who live here work in the creative industries, in advertising and graphic design, and commute to Copenhagen most days. They were both quite worried about leaving the stimulating lifestyle they had in the city behind them, but neither of them has regretted their decision.

Vedbæk, where the house is located, is a picturesque village by the sea, with beaches and a harbour a stone's throw away – the family soon discovered that the lack of nightlife and shopping was more than made up for by the possibility of popping around the corner to buy fresh fish straight off the boats.

The house was originally built as a summer-house in 1924, with an extended living room and first floor attached a few years later. But it is just as suitable as a year-round abode, with a lush garden showing the passing of the seasons.

The ground floor has been turned into a thoroughly modern open-plan space, with views through the front room to the kitchen and the garden beyond – the doors are left open for as long as the weather allows.

Originally, the flooring was covered in tatty carpets, but when they were peeled back, lovely floorboards were unearthed that were then sanded and varnished throughout the space. In a typically modern, Scandinavian way, the windows are unobstructed by curtains or blinds to let as much light in as possible, and the cozy factor stems from an open fire, book-lined walls and good lighting.

The walls of the living room are lined with bespoke shelves, which were created specifically for this room by Copenhagen design bureau Design By Us. You would never guess that these shelves were new though, what with the bottom cupboards looking like they were built at the same time as the house – a good trick to update old houses is to build modern storage solutions using reclaimed materials.

The simple but supremely comfortable sofas are from Italian furniture company Moroso, and the stylish chrome lamps are from classic French company Jieldé. Simple flowers in small bunches dotted around the shelving soften the hard lines of the books and shelves. There are plenty of Danish design classics to be found around the house, along with a canvas and leather easy chair that is very similar to the Spanish chair designed by Börge Mogensen.

The office space is one of the family's favourite rooms, with its clean lines and functional furniture. The desk also came from Design By Us and was custom-built – its yellow hue really lifts the room and is a great colour for getting you in the right mood for work. It also has a large amount of space for your legs underneath, a factor that's sometimes overlooked in a home office. The chair on castors is an Arne

ABOVE A bright accent in a workspace can really stimulate the senses, and a hit of yellow is perfect for when the weather is gloomy and grey. **LEFT** The family really loves the kitchen, with its unusual, high-gloss carved units created by Design by Us and light colours. The wooden floorboards are comfortable underfoot.

The ground floor has been
turned into a thoroughly
modern open–plan space with
a roaring fire to keep it warm.

THIS PAGE The dining room melds old and new, with a vintage chandelier hanging perfectly above a sleek table and chairs. The recess is an original feature. The vintage Eiffel chairs are by Charles and Ray Eames – the way to know that they are original is whether they are made out of fibreglass rather than plastic. **OPPOSITE** The nook by the fire is a favourite place to spend time in winter; the artwork mirrors the flames even when the fire is not lit.

BELOW LEFT The squashy outdoor seat comes from Danish company Karmameju, which specializes in furniture used outdoors that breaks traditional moulds. The large olive tree provides a Mediterranean feel to the space. **BELOW CENTRE** The family entertains

outside whenever the sun rears its head – it's the perfect spot for afternoon coffee and a Danish or two. **BELOW RIGHT** Simple peonies look beautiful in a plain vase, and even more so set against the weather-beaten clapperboard that is typical of the area.

Jacobsen original – the wheels make it easy for whoever sits in it to swish around and pick up papers or put back folders. A selection of personal mementos has been put on the wall, providing a place to rest your eyes when work takes its toll.

In the large kitchen, the family gathers for meals and to spend time together. The unusual white units came about when the lady of the house saw a pattern on a wallpaper that she loved, but wasn't keen to put paper on the wall. Instead, Design By Us came up with the idea of carving the pattern onto the cabinetry and to then add several coats of glossy paint to give it lustre and sheen. The carvings mirror the effect of light and shadow beautifully throughout the day. The large green tiles break up the white space, and although they are made from Sicilian lava stone, they feel strangely at home here due to their rustic surface.

The family often entertains at home, which most people in the Nordic countries tend to do rather than eat out in large groups at a restaurant, as is often the case in Mediterranean countries. To cope with big parties, there are two sinks in the kitchen, making it easier to wash up a large stack of dishes.

The veranda outside makes a great place to relax. Olive trees grow happily in the garden along with thyme, jasmine, lavender, clematis and roses, creating beautifully scented summer evenings. The wooden furniture is made by a traditional manufacturer and can be found in many Danish gardens – like the rest of the house it is built to last, but without being heavy or clunky. This feeling permeates the home. Filled with design classics, it could feel burdened by tradition, but instead the young family who live here have proved that true style always stands the test of time.

THIS PAGE The veranda works as a wonderful extension to the living room, giving fresh life to the 'bringing the outside in' concept. The balcony above it has enviable sea views. A white tablecloth and terracotta pots show the family's love of the simple things in life.

eclectic
harmony

Lars Kristensen's home in Copenhagen is not a conversion but part of a 19th-century purpose-built apartment block. When Lars bought the apartment in 1998, it had been lived in by the same family for 30 years prior to that. The apartment is typically Danish in that the main reception rooms run along the front and a long corridor links these rooms and the bedrooms at the back with the kitchen and what would once have been the servants' quarters, away from the rest of the living space.

Lars acquired the apartment in a hurry. Having viewed it only once, he bought it overnight, after leaving a phone message to say that he wanted to take it. When he went to visit the apartment again, he noticed how dark it was, with lowered ceilings and the glassed parts of the internal doors boarded over, but he could also see that it had potential. Although the interior was very dark, its position on the top floor of the building meant that it could receive maximum natural light from three sides – the building is on a corner.

Nevertheless, the apartment as a whole felt like a tightly closed parcel. 'I knew that I would

ABOVE Displaying a quirky and comfortable taste, Lars has combined any number of styles and periods to harmonious and undeniably Scandinavian effect, from the 18th-century dining table to the 20th-century metal prison chairs. **OPPOSITE** From the dining room there are views through to the sitting room and to the central corridor with Lars's office beyond. Although there is a sense of space, there is also an easy and logical flow between the different areas and a fluent coherence in the interior design.

RIGHT The dark, narrow hall is typical of old Danish apartment buildings of this age. Layers of paper were removed from the glass panels above the doors to bring some much-needed light into the centre of the space.

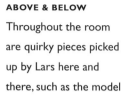

ABOVE & BELOW Throughout the room are quirky pieces picked up by Lars here and there, such as the model of a theatre interior, formerly used by hotel concierges to indicate the position of seats to possible patrons.

have to unwrap it to get down to the real thing, and I wasn't sure what I'd find when I got there,' says Lars. 'I couldn't see what might be within. So I acquired it rapidly, but since I didn't have the money to do it all at once, I then had to assemble it slowly.'

The first rooms that he attacked were the living areas, his office and his bedroom. 'There were three painters here for a month, peeling off ten layers of wall and ceiling paper, removing the boards from the glass sections of the internal doors, as well as restoring and lightening the floors.' There are no rugs in the apartment – Lars doesn't need them or see the point of them.

To open up the apartment further, Lars removed the door between the hall and the dining room, and then created visual links between this room and the living room beyond

THIS PAGE The living room
is a combination of comfort
and classicism. On the far
wall, a striking work by Maibritt
Ulvedal Bjelke injects colour
into what is otherwise a neutral
palette with nothing to disturb
the neutral, calm tones of
furniture, walls and floor.

it. To lead the eye onwards, he painted the two rooms in similar tones. Although some might think it unusual today to have a separate dining room, in Lars's hands it is very much part of the general living area. As he says, 'It doesn't feel cut off from the rest of the apartment and if — as I do — you have twelve people to dinner five times a year, then it is worth having; indeed, it's very nice to have.'

On the right-hand side of the corridor is his office, 'the centre of the apartment', from where one can see in several directions at once, and that leads into the bedroom. This room is neat, clean and rather functional. One door leads into the small bathroom, which Lars tackled three years after the first renovation, and that is now bereft of its gaudy orange and brown tiles, finished instead with all-white ones. This room is a good example of Lars's enduring need to match the functional with the aesthetic. 'While aesthetics are important to me, I realize that we need functional things to sustain ordinary life,' he says. 'I have to shower and wash, for example — but I would still rather

THIS PAGE The final part of the apartment to be converted by Lars, the kitchen was created out of three small, irregular rooms that included the servants' quarters. It is now a large working and dining kitchen in which the cooking and utility area is concentrated at one end of the room, with a simple breakfast table at the other. The two are linked by a decorative painted table pushed up against the wall to give more space.

The colours used in the decor of the apartment are equally low-key. 'Copenhagen doesn't have much light, so you need to add as much as you can through the walls,' says Lars. 'I always go for soft-washed colours, including light grey. I like a contrast between the walls and the much stronger colours of the artworks. It's a sort of mixture of Swedish and French with a touch of English.'

The apartment is perfect for Lars. 'For my way of life, I need a retreat from the fuss and noise of the street, so I must have around me a few well-chosen things. What I enjoy is the architectural feeling of the apartment, and the knowledge that I didn't need to add much to the original.'

have a good-looking shower, and even if it does splash water a bit, I would rather dry the floor than have an ugly shower.'

What is now the kitchen was, when he found the flat, three rooms, one of them a maid's room. Now it is a pleasing, light room, one end devoted to the mechanics of cooking and cleaning, the other to the pleasures of dining, with a small, old table and chairs and a bench in the window.

Many of the objects in the apartment are antique, while the artworks are modern. 'I like the mixture,' says Lars. 'In the dining room is a chandelier from a Swedish castle, an 18th-century wooden table and 20th-century metal chairs, originally made for prison use.' Lars looks out for objects that combine function and decoration – in the sitting room, a metal cabinet that he found in a shipyard houses all the stereo equipment. All the furnishings are simple and there are few curtains; some chairs are covered with basic ticking; others with white linen sheets. It's an interesting mixture, but one that appears deceptively simple – in reality, it is a difficult look to achieve and it's hard to create the right juxtaposition of hard and soft.

Vintage–inspired

Retro, second-hand, vintage, salvage – these are just some of the words used to describe furniture and accessories that aren't brand new. In fact, many of the most beautiful vintage items to be found have been around the block a few times. Instead of making them less attractive, this is what gives them that special *je ne sais quoi*. The Scandinavians are very fond of mixing old and new, welcoming antiques into their home. Yet you don't need to spend a lot of money on these items – shabby and worn things take on a patina all of their own when displayed with love and they give the home a unique look. Think dull, silvery tones, frayed edges and scuffed paintwork for a look that has its very own kind of beauty.

swedish vintage

ABOVE LEFT Even the cats get a stylish place to sleep in Nina's house. The glass doors hail from an old ribbon shop and were carefully brought back from France.
ABOVE RIGHT The matte silver of the lamp and stools sits well with the white tongue-and-groove walls, adding texture to the pale colours. **OPPOSITE** The kitchen is the heart of this home, with its calming colours and shabby-chic feel. The distinctive chairs are made by the classic French brand, Tolix.

In Nina Hartmann's house, old and shabby furniture means one thing – beauty. Her five-bedroom house in southern Sweden is filled with things that other people have thrown away or sold because they were a bit worn out or no longer modern. But in Nina's eyes, this is what makes these objects special: 'I don't care for new things made to look vintage. I love old things with charm and a bit of history behind them.'

But despite the magpie attitude behind Nina's style, her house exudes a sense of relaxed calm. It is filled with soothing shades of white and grey; from the scuffed, painted furniture to the matte silver on candlesticks and lampshades. These colours reflect the light of southern Sweden, where the short winter days and long summer evenings carry a quality that is mirrored by these calming interiors.

ABOVE The baskets are made from hand-woven strips of bark, which was a common skill in Sweden only a few generations back. Using fabric instead of doors on your cupboards is a quick and cheap way to update your kitchen, and a good way of adding both colour and texture.

It is hard to imagine that this house is only nine years old. The Hartmann family built it from scratch, and have since extended it and refurbished the kitchen and bathroom. It is also hard to imagine that there are five children and six cats sharing the space with Nina and her husband Tore. But the house copes well with a large family, mainly due to its vintage fittings — there is not a lot the children can do to them that they haven't already suffered.

Nina's love of all things old extends to her job as a stylist, and to her online shop. It is a treasure trove of antique linen, old architectural finds and her own speciality —

ABOVE French wire baskets make an exciting contrast with the white walls in the kitchen, while the steel Tolix chair adds a rustic air. The garden can be glimpsed through the wide-open doors, which makes it easy to enjoy a meal outside.

mercury-glassed silver. She calls this 'poor man's silver' and is on a constant lookout for it on her excursions to car boot sales and local auctions in the neighbouring villages. Even the six cats have their own collection of silver candlesticks, artfully grouped on a shelf above their basket.

The look of the house is unified by its white colour scheme – all of the walls are white, although some are clad in tongue and groove, which instantly lends a country air to a room. The wide, pale floorboards further enhance the rural feel, and make the house seem much older than it is. Most old Scandinavian houses have similarly wide floorboards, often taken from a forest growing just outside. This has the effect of connecting Nina's house to the roots of the area, despite it being a new build.

Nina has put her personal stamp on every corner of the house, giving it a tantalizing mix of Swedish and French country chic. Apart from scouring local auctions, Nina also travels to France and Belgium to pick up good-quality linen and furniture at low prices. The linen, which is often beautifully embroidered and monogrammed, is then transformed into cushions, pillowcases and serviettes, adding a further authentic touch to the interior that can only be achieved by using antique linen.

In the master bedroom, a lovely French metal double bed is given a modern touch by the stencilled words on the wall above it – these are excerpts from Danish poetry.

The kitchen has an assortment of white-painted chairs, tables and sideboards, which all look artfully distressed. But part of the charm of this house is that it is not contrived or manufactured. 'I bought it looking like this, already a bit shabby – I love the shabby-chic style,' says Nina.

Materials like the rough, powder-coated steel of the classic Tolix chairs and stools break up the whiteness of the room

ABOVE The living room is decorated in relaxing colours, and the chairs invite you to sit down and daydream in front of the wide windows. The vintage candlestick in the window is of a traditional French style, and its black ironwork patterns stand out in contrast to the pale colours of the room. Not having curtains is important in a culture that adores light. Houses in Sweden tend to be well set apart, which means that privacy is maintained.

RIGHT Floral patterns are introduced carefully and can be mixed freely, as they all share the same base colours. Nina's love of 'poor man's silver' can be seen in the containers on the shelf and the shimmering lampshade. **BELOW** A little nook for playing, reading or drawing is great for the kids — tidying up also becomes a breeze with the handy drawstring bags hanging from hooks, while the farm animals have a good view from the hand-woven basket. The board with ribbons displays photographs and postcards that can be changed around according to one's mood.

and give it depth. Further touches that underline the simplicity of the house's interior are the wire baskets that hang from the kitchen wall. 'This type of craft is called fil de fer in France, and the baskets are normally used for gathering eggs,' says Nina.

Another material that Nina loves is a Swedish speciality — birch bark woven into strips to create baskets and hampers. The baskets are available from local craftsmen, in antiques shops or at auctions. The fine wood grain in the strips contrasts beautifully with the white cabinetry, and gives it an air of a traditional country kitchen. Such old artefacts are also a reminder of the days before the advent of creature comforts such as central heating and electricity. The dark Nordic winters used to force people to spend the evenings indoors creating household items that were as beautiful as they were useful — a creative past that is often not more than a few generations away from today's modern Scandinavians.

THIS PAGE An old post office sorting
shelf works well for modern books.
On the trestle table, fabric-clad boxes
add some floral joy, while the Tolix chairs
keep the rustic theme going strong.

Tre små engle skal følge dig,
på livets vej herned.
Den ene tro.
Den anden håb.
Den tredje kærlighed.

THIS PAGE In one of the children's rooms, an antique horse on wheels watches over the bed. The plain Roman blind is a good foil against the rosebuds on the bedspread, and stops the room being too cute. A Danish poem on the wall provides daily inspiration.

The living room houses the only modern furniture in the home – the sofas from Ikea. But despite being new, they blend into the calm, clean feel of the room due to their classic design and oatmeal-coloured coverings. Nina has placed one of her favourite items in the house, a black metal candlestick, in the large windows. 'This type of candleholder comes from French churches, where they are specifically lit during the harvest festivals as a thank-you for the bountiful harvests. And, of course, they are rather old,' says Nina.

Although it might not be noticeable at first, there are touches of black in all the rooms to keep the white, grey and neutral colours grounded: in the kitchen it's the wire baskets, in the bedroom another French candlestick, in the living room the lettering on the cushions and in the bathroom a black and white chequered-floor. These splashes of black are important, as they work as a foil for the lighter colours and stop them looking washed out.

When it comes to modern Scandinavian designers, Nina is unsurprisingly not a huge fan. She does like the work of Poul Henningsen and his PH lamp, but has chosen a Bestlite floor lamp for her own living room. 'It was designed in the 1930s, so it can hardly be called modern. And Churchill had one, so if it was good enough for him...' Nina says. And like everything else in this relaxed, comforting house, even the Bestlite seems to have found its very own natural place to be.

ABOVE In the master bedroom, a giant antique French bed takes pride of place with its high mattress. The windows have shutters rather than fabric curtains to keep the room uncluttered.
LEFT The bathroom is modern, but with a vintage feel. The ornate antique candleholder makes the act of taking a bath all the more enticingly romantic.

salvaging the past

Scandinavians have strong feelings when it comes to environmental awareness, with recycling high on everybody's agenda. But not everyone has built their entire house of salvaged materials like Martin Nannestad Jørgensen has. From the walls and windows to the floorboards, every scrap has been reclaimed and reused, with fantastic results.

'I started my project in 1985,' says Martin. 'Some friends and I used to perform salvage raids on torn-down buildings in Copenhagen to try to preserve some of the lovely things that would otherwise have been destroyed. I started by getting the doors and windows, and it all kind of followed on from there.'

The house consists of a large studio space, where Martin works as a textile designer and weaver, a bathroom, a large open-plan kitchen-cum-living area and a sleeping space.

Like the house, the furniture is also salvaged from different countries and places – one of Martin's chairs was found in a skip in Provence, another was picked up at an old hospital in Greenland, while his grandparents left him a design classic in the form of a Wegner chair.

ABOVE There's no such thing as a useless piece in this house – Martin's eye can create a beautiful still life with things other people would place in a skip. **OPPOSITE** The house is completely made up of recycled materials. Martin grew up in Greenland, where the large skull resting on the blue metal beam came from.

THIS PAGE The kitchen is simple but functional, filled with salvaged pieces. The ladder is needed to open and close the high window.

ABOVE The selection of vintage knives is on hand when Martin cooks, perhaps rustling up one of his famous rhubarb crumbles.
ABOVE & BELOW RIGHT The 1950s coat hooks are used as a place to hang kitchen towels rather than clothing. Just off the kitchen, an old medicine cabinet provides plenty of storage for bits and bobs – of course, this is another of Martin's finds, salvaged rather than shopped for. The CD collection houses music from all over the world, but jazz is a prevailing favourite.

In the middle of the ceiling in the studio hangs a globe, reminding Martin of his many long travels around the world. He grew up in Greenland, but soon developed a desire for globetrotting. His native land is still present in the form of the animal skulls scattered around the house, which he gets from Greenland – the slightly menacing, large cranium above the blue steel beam is that of a killer whale. It might not be to everyone's taste, but certainly sparks conversation.

Instead of painting the whole space white, Martin has left some panels in the studio in untreated wood, to stop the room becoming too uniform and ascetic. The randomness of the wood also creates an exciting tension in the room and encourages the eye to wander around it.

Across the space runs a washing line, which could be used for displaying artworks and pegging up mementoes, but that more often than not is used for its original purpose – drying wet clothes.

In Martin's eyes, everything can become an object of beauty. Above the old Ikea sofa hangs a square of white-enamelled metal where the rust has created patterns that take on a life of their own when you look at them for long enough.

On top of the old cupboard with its white, panelled doors lies a collection of drawings, old maps and pieces of pretty wrapping paper; tucked away but not forgotten. Postcards and other pieces of memorabilia have been stuck in under the door frame for display purposes and to inspire those who pass by it.

ABOVE & ABOVE LEFT If they could speak, the old toy lorries would have some stories to tell – they were made by inmates in a Danish prison. The dining table is actually a drawing table from an architect's office and is height-adjustable, which makes it good for multi-tasking – great for dinner parties and equally useful for work.
LEFT Hooks play home to assorted kitchen tools – no Nordic home is complete without a cheese slice.

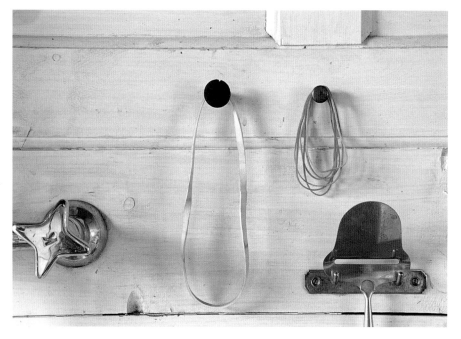

Instead of painting the whole space white, Martin has left some panels in untreated wood, to stop the room becoming too uniform.

The wooden board with little metal pegs is actually an antique thresher, which Martin found in central Spain. 'The farmers used to tie it behind a mule who dragged it through the wheat to separate it from the chaff. Little children used to sit on it to make it heavier.' But true to his love of salvage, he didn't buy it. 'I managed to trade it for one of my polar bear skulls from Greenland,' smiles Martin.

A simple selection of furniture gets an almost still-life quality when put together carefully. The old motoring sign was picked up from a deserted railway station in southern France, while the drawers underneath were the only salvageable parts of a bigger piece. A colourful olive-oil tin has been turned into a bin.

The hippo is a replica of an ancient Egyptian original, which is on display at the Glyptotek museum, Copenhagen. The white piece of marble and the granite was used for making paint, by rubbing it over colour pigments and linseed oil to create a paste and then paint.

Although mainly there for decoration, the old window-cleaning ladder is also used to access the area above the bathroom. The kitchen is basic, but used frequently when Martin is entertaining. One of his favourite ingredients is rhubarb, which he turns into a crumble with a secret ingredient in the topping: marzipan. 'And plenty of it!' says Martin.

A shallow, white wooden floor shelf makes a good storage space for the plentiful music collection – Miles Davis is a particular favourite of Martin's. The colourful clothes hooks used in the kitchen are inspired by the Eameses' Hang It All that were manufactured in Belgium and Holland in the 1950s.

BELOW The timeless chair is a mix of art deco influences and mid-century modernism. The cushion is made from a blanket picked up in Bolivia on one of Martin's many travels.

BELOW LEFT The coat hooks provide a jolt of colour against the blue background and were inspired by legendary design duo Ray and Charles Eames's Hang It All. A bag provides useful extra storage. BELOW CENTRE The sofa was purchased from Ikea, and has lasted well – its slightly worn look makes it fit with its surroundings. The 'artwork' on the wall is actually a piece of metal where the corrosion has created an exciting pattern. The washing line strung across the room can also be used to peg up photos and other mementoes. BELOW RIGHT The wall-mounted anglepoise can be used for task lighting or to set the evening mood by raising the beam towards the ceiling. OPPOSITE The unusual wooden item is an old thresher from Spain, which gets a sculptural aspect when hung on the wall. The top of the cupbooard is a good spot to store rolled-up maps and drawings – more like a bank of inspiration than just a hideaway.

Matching colours help the magpie collection of salvaged goods hang together in the house. By rights, the place should be a big old recycled mess, but by sticking to certain colours, like the pale blue of the medicine cabinet on the wall echoed in the storage box and kitchen towel, Martin has achieved a harmonious look in his home.

The dining table is an old drawing table of the type that would often be found in architects' offices. It has a pedal to raise and lower it, making it multi-functional. The large, ceiling-mounted light is from a hospital in Thule, Greenland – Martin says it's perfect, as it doesn't get hot and spreads an even and shadow-free light. On the table is a candlestick holder made from porcelain isolators that were taken from a radio mast in Greenland.

On the beams, vintage toy trucks have been parked as decorations. They were inherited from Martin's grandparents and were manufactured by inmates in Danish prisons. The stylish chair in metal and leather, found in an antiques shop, is home to a cushion made from a blanket picked up in Bolivia. On one of the retro coat hooks Martin has placed a blue and white-striped bag that works as a washing basket and lends a nautical feel to the area.

Because of Martin's need for light when he works, the studio is built with large windows and skylights. And perhaps it is this craving for light together with its ecological credentials that make this a typically Scandinavian home – it is certainly the perfect place to come home to after roaming the globe looking for treasures.

THIS PAGE Set against the calming grey walls, the global souvenirs create a beautiful still life. And despite their cultural differences, the objects get along: the head-dress is from South Africa, while the chest is Chinese. The shabby-chic side table that holds the scheme together is from New York.

worldly surrounds

ABOVE LEFT Lars's living room is a cosmopolitan mix of Scandinavian colours and exotic patterns. The prints above the sofa are from India, the sequinned cushions from Morocco and the zebra was bagged by a friend of Lars. The tiled oven in the corner is a traditional and incredibly efficient Nordic way of heating.

ABOVE RIGHT The sofas were custom-built for this family space, where the Wibergs eat, play and work. The rattan baskets are useful for hiding clutter.

The Danes have long been seafaring folk and the country has strong maritime bonds, from the old Vikings to present-day shipping tycoons. Modern Danes might steer clear of a longship when they go on vacation, but the wanderlust is still strong – and nowhere is this as clear as in fashion shop owner Lars Wiberg's home.

This house outside Copenhagen is filled with colours and textures that are far removed from the pale Scandinavian palette. Rajasthani pinks and oranges sit comfortably next to Russian floral patterns, and African tribal art shares space with Chinese antiques. But instead of creating a riot of clashing colours, the neutral walls and clean-lined furniture provide a calming influence, and make sure that statement pieces have the chance to really stand out.

The house was built in 1900, and when Lars moved in with his family he had to start from scratch with the renovations. But it was worth it, as the building could offer the most priceless of commodities in the Nordic countries: 'It was the light that drew us here,' says Lars. The rooms are spacious and well laid out, with beautiful wooden parquet in some areas and white, glossy floorboards in others.

Through the large windows you can glimpse the garden, which is the family's pride and joy. In the warmer months they spend a lot of their waking time in it, entertaining or just enjoying the all-too-short Scandinavian summer.

When the weather takes a turn for the worse, the Wibergs get together for meals around the large table in the dining room. This is perhaps the most international room in the house, although it's not the most colourful – the heavy wooden table and chairs are from Syria, the Buddha in the window is Chinese and the elegant curtains were picked up in Paris. But the rather Mexican-looking vase housing a cactus is actually a home-grown design, by Danish company Day Birger et Mikkelsen.

ABOVE & RIGHT Having a white space makes it easy to add accent colours. This hallway feels bright and airy thanks to the colourful accessories from around the world, mirrored in the berry-coloured rug. When the colour scheme starts feeling tired, or even when the seasons change and darker, cozier colours are needed, it is easy with such a neutral background to change the accessories for a whole new look. In the children's room, a clothes cupboard gets turned into a cabinet of curiosities with its unusual mix of patterns and colour.

THIS PAGE The dining room
is cool and sophisticated, with
a truly international flavour.
The cacti are reminiscent of
South America, the heavy table
is from Syria and the Buddha
breathes a Zen-like calm over
mealtime. The meals served
in this room are also infused
with global ingredients.

The grey walls of the dining room mirror those in the living space, where squishy, cream-coloured sofas stand out against the darker backdrop. 'The sofas aren't terribly exclusive; they're from Ikea,' says Lars. 'We prefer to buy new ones often, when they get grubby.' The sofas may be new, but the chandelier certainly isn't; it's an old French antique. The blanket edged with feathers is also French, and the animal textures are echoed in the zebra skin on the floor.

'That has rather a special story behind it,' says Lars, 'as a friend of ours actually shot the zebra!'

THIS PAGE The global theme continues in the bedroom, with the elegant colour scheme holding the artefacts together. The Moroccan bedlinen and rug have plenty of sequins to add sparkle, while the African objects at the foot of the bed offer an earthier feel. The skin of a python runs above the bed.

Having stories behind furniture and items is very important to the Wibergs, and they'd much rather pick something up on one of their travels than buy it from a shop. The bedroom, for example, is adorned with the creamy textiles embellished with sparkling sequins typical of Morocco, while the patterned framed item above the bed is actually a python skin. The lamp and the mirror were bought in St Tropez. 'We travel all the time – it gives us life,' says Lars, 'and it also provides endless inspiration.'

The hallway opens out onto the lush garden, where the global theme is continued with a mix of exotic plants and more sedately Danish varieties. African and Asian souvenirs make the white hallway exciting, and the pink stripes of the rug lift the spirits.

In little Liva's room the colours sparkle, with the strong pinks and oranges of India being a recurring theme. 'We love India,

ABOVE LEFT The washroom is light and feminine – it's a place where Lars's wife Camilla enjoys spending time. **ABOVE RIGHT** The bathroom comes in a dark, dramatic mahogany wood, making it feel a lot like a boutique hotel – this is not only a room to get clean in but a place to relax, recharge and spend quality time. **LEFT** Scraps of shiny, glittering materials serve as inspiration for Lars in his job in the fashion industry, and look lovely against the worn surface of the chest that sits behind them.

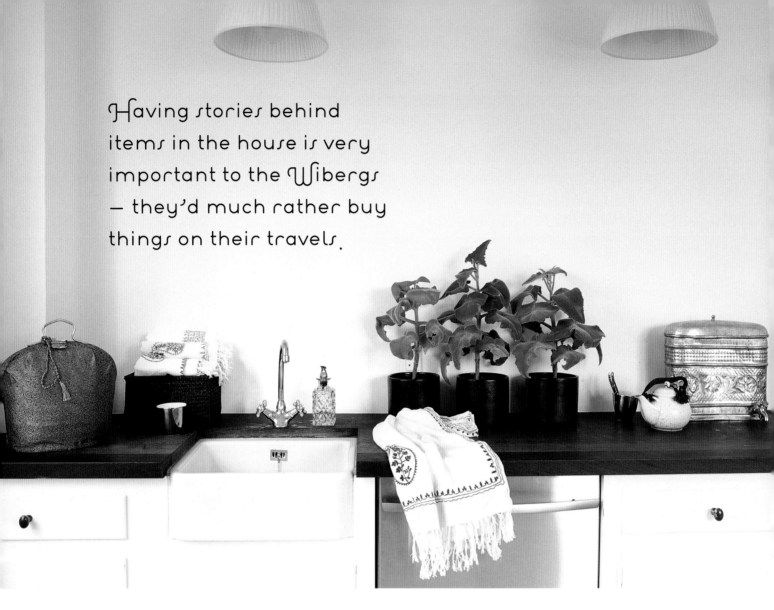

Having stories behind items in the house is very important to the Wibergs — they'd much rather buy things on their travels.

especially Rajasthan,' says Lars. 'The colours there really make you dream and are flavoured by life.'

The additional seating area is where the family gathers for less formal meals and other fun activities. The trotting camel picture is by a local painter, while the chair with inlaid mother-of-pearl is from Day Birger et Mikkelsen.

There might not be an abundance of classic Danish furniture in the house, but this is something the family is planning to change. 'In future, we'll be buying more home-grown furniture. Danish designers have a fantastic way of keeping their lines pure,' says Lars.

Simple seating units at the dining table were custom-built for the space, and house some useful baskets where the Wibergs store candles and other items that don't need to be on display.

In the kitchen, the white units have a Shaker look to them, a style that borrows a lot of aspects from traditional Scandinavian furniture. The carefully selected items really stand out against the light kitchen walls, while the dark-wood worktop stops the area feeling washed out. Lars takes great care with the small items that surround him, like the fabric tea cosy — perhaps the prayer beads he has attached to it are a silent plea that the pot will never run dry.

OPPOSITE The kitchen is a mix of exotica and minimalism, with clean lines and objects all mixed up. The Belfast sink gives it a traditional feel, while the silver accents and Turkish hammam towel keep it in line with the international theme throughout the house.

THIS PAGE Concrete can be used beautifully in the right setting. In the garden, deep daybeds have been built in an L-shape for guests to be able to relax and chat together easily.

The colour scheme in the bathroom is as dark as the kitchen is bright, with panelling and bath surround in a dark mahogany. Some people hesitate to use wood in wet areas, but treated correctly, hardwoods will last for many a year in contact with water – after all, up until recently this is the material all ships were made from. The hammam towels are from Morocco, and Lars loves them – as opposed to thicker towelling versions, these dry you really efficiently and also take a shorter time to get dry on a towel warmer.

In all, the bathroom with its contrasting colour schemes and spa-like calm is one of the couple's favourite places. 'We light candles in here, get the essential oils out and get in the bath together. It makes the evenings so relaxing.'

Concrete might not be to everyone's taste when it comes to garden materials, but the Wibergs' low couches for entertaining fit surprisingly well in the setting. The family loves cooking and tries to have friends over every second weekend. Lars's favourite treat for his guests is to theme the evening: 'They love it!'

And when it comes to themes, the one pervading this house is that, although travel is inspiring and exciting, it is not the be all and end all – it's the coming home that counts.

THIS PAGE The house has come a long way since its original use as a stables. The open-plan living area is divided by a glass wall to maximize light, while the interior is a charming mix of old furniture and modern stainless steel. **OPPOSITE** Anja's collection of antique angels brightens up the walls with their faded lustre.

antique
& modern

History is ever present in this Copenhagen house, both in the carefully selected objects and the building itself. When antiques dealer Anja Alfieri moved in 10 years ago, it was little more than a ruin, but she and her partner saw its potential and acted on it.

'This was originally a stable, built in 1903, but later on it housed some of the first cars to be imported into Denmark,' she says. Its unusual beginnings are still evident in the high ceilings and open-plan living space on the first floor, while downstairs Anja has her quirky antiques shop.

Most of the furniture and items in the house are on constant rotation, and if customers want to buy them, almost everything is for sale. But Anja doesn't mind, as there are always further finds to display and incorporate into her home. She has a special knack for mixing objects from different cultures, and finding uses for them that aren't immediately

obvious – an old Japanese water bucket is turned into
a container for firewood, while a former kitchen cabinet
sits happily in the bathroom.

Despite its vintage furnishings, the home has a
surprisingly fresh feel to it, due to the painstaking care
with which Anja selects its contents. The white walls
enhance this fresh feel further still. All of the wooden
floorboards are painted pale white in the house, which lets
your eye wander through the space and allows the numerous
antiques to do the talking. The walls are adorned with
antique paintings and mirrors, many of which are gilded in
old gold. 'I really like the faded quality of them, while new
gold would just be too shiny,' says Anja.

LEFT The Chinese cabinet sits
well with the antique angels
above – the fact that they are
showing signs of wear and tear
adds to their charm. The old
ladder is handy when it comes
to cleaning the skylights.

ABOVE The vintage stove works
as well now as the day it was
made, and is a focal point during
winter. The chairs have been left
scuffed and untreated on
purpose, which makes them
more, rather than less, beautiful.

Much of the furniture has been customized by Anja,
like the low sofas made from vintage French mattresses and
placed on castors sourced from a local scaffolding company
(although her dream sofa is one made by Danish designer
Kaare Klint). The bright look is further enhanced by the light
streaming in from the skylights, which Anja had put in when
she renovated the house. 'Our home is in an inner courtyard
close to the Amalienborg Palace, and though we have a small
space outside to enjoy, we needed light from above as well,'
she says. 'So now we can spend time lying on the floor in the
evenings, just looking out at the moon and the stars.'

The portraits adorning the walls in the bedroom and living space date mostly from the 18th century, and although Anja doesn't know the names of the people depicted in them, she likes to have the paintings around her. 'They are really cozy,' she says, 'and they all tell a story of real people from a time gone by.'

One of her other passions is collecting gold angels. These are seen scattered around the space, some of them with an arm or a leg missing (or both). They create an impact on the walls, due to their 3D qualities, which is one of Anja's favourite ways to introduce texture and excitement into a room. She finds her antiques and vintage items both at home in Copenhagen (she especially recommends the shop Greensquare) and while travelling in France.

She also has a fondness for South-East Asian furniture, like the red-lacquered Chinese cabinet and the Japanese water bucket, which sit comfortably with the examples of Danish design in the home – the pale, simple shapes of Scandinavian furniture often work very well with the clean lines and natural materials that are synonymous with Japanese design.

The kitchen is separated from the main living area by a glass wall, which cuts out the sound of clattering pans and cooking smells, but still lets the light through and increases the feeling of openness. And if the rest of the house is filled with antiques, the kitchen is unashamedly modern with stainless-steel appliances and units filling the space.

THIS PAGE Stainless steel is a practical option for kitchen surfaces, and keeps the area light. Adding vintage utensils and old pictures stops the kitchen from looking cold and clinical. Washing up is less of a chore when you have old Copenhagen to gaze out onto while you do it – lighting a candle makes the task almost seem a pleasure.

ABOVE Part of the original machinery has been left in the study, and provides an interesting talking point. The sleek computer has been placed on a white tablecloth to continue the mix of old and new in the home.
OPPOSITE A candlelit dinner under the eaves of the old stable is a fine treat. The shabby-chic chairs and textured tablecloth stop the table looking too formal.

'Cooking is very important to me,' says Anja. 'Maybe it's because I'm half Italian, but I love it and cook every day.'

The sleek, stainless-steel units are broken up by square tiles that function as an extra-high splashback, and add that vintage feel which Anja loves. An old crate works as extra storage on top of the fridge, while the unusual snake poster is an educational picture sourced from an old school in Sweden – perhaps not an obvious choice for a kitchen, but the shape of the snake works well with the spindly wire tools and containers hanging underneath it. And to stop the space from feeling too clinical, Anja has added a crystal chandelier and a selection of candlesticks which that up the area on dark winter nights. The washing up is done in front of the tall windows, looking out on the old Copenhagen façades opposite.

The bathroom is an equal mix of modern comforts and vintage coziness. The walk-in shower is screened off by a modern frosted-glass panel, while the roll-top bathtub rests snugly on a mosaic floor. The bathroom has a similar feel to a 1930s public swimming pool. 'My partner Jesper used to swim competitively when he was young, so he spent most of his youth in the local swimming pool,' laughs Anja. 'He feels right at home here!'

The bedroom is calm and soothing, with Anja's trademark oil portrait and castored bed taking pride of place. The exposed beams have been left untreated to give a reminder of the

Despite its vintage furnishings, there is a surprisingly fresh feel to this home, due to the care with which its contents have been chosen.

history of the house, and the wooden floors carry through the simple style from the rest of the home.

On the internal window ledge to the bedroom is a selection of miniature Tolix chairs, which the French travelling salesmen used to carry with them to show off their wares.

Outside the bedroom is an unusual memento: an old tree stump that is used as a casual side table for an antique lamp. It was brought back from the little village in Germany where Anja's mother was born after World War II, and apart from showing Anja's skill in using items in an unusual manner, it also carries its past effortlessly, making it sit perfectly in this home where history is always present.

RIGHT Putting castors on your bed is both a practical and stylish option. **BELOW** The bathroom has a decidedly retro feel, due to its square white tiles and deep, roll-top bathtub.

BELOW RIGHT The shower screen is very modern and has the look of a contemporary wet-room – as a former swimmer, Anja's partner feels totally at home here.

Pared-down Modern

Scandinavian modernity is often about reworking themes and materials already in use.
Where the Italians had the bright primary colours of Ettore Sottsass, the Nordic countries
produced the striking but simple lines and shades of Arne Jacobsen and Alvar Aalto.
Modernity in itself might not be a look that most Scandinavians strive for, but the quest for
a contemporary way of life often comes through in spacious architecture, functional
furniture and light materials. Typical ways to create modern spaces and items are to use an
old material or technique in a new way. In the following pages you'll see traditional wood
cladding that has created a hyper-new façade or a woven basket that is firmly 'now'.

LEFT The pine theme continues outside the house with a large expanse of decking that is complemented by a simple set of table and chairs – perfect for outdoor dining.
OPPOSITE Floor-to-ceiling windows maximize the amount of light.
BELOW LEFT The dining table and chairs are by Alvar Aalto and were designed in the 1930s.

rural retreat

The Suppanen house – called Villa Ilo – is in the Åland archipelago, between Finland and Sweden, and is reached from the harbour city of Turku in western Finland. The area is popular with sailors and visitors alike, but although it is a haven in summer, the winters can be very demanding. Villa Ilo is unique in its curving form, which was designed to follow the shape of the land and complement the cliff-top location. The house was built for relatives of the architect and designer Ilkka Suppanen.

Suppanen studied architecture at the Technical University of Helsinki, and interior and furniture design at the University of Art and Design Helsinki. In 1995, he founded Studio Suppanen in Helsinki. His clients include Artek, Axis, Cappellini, Ferlea, Lucente, Luhta, Nokia, Proventus and Saab. He was also one of the founders of the Snowcrash collective. Suppanen was rewarded in 2006 with the Bruno Mathsson prize, the most prestigious design

award in Sweden. The Villa Ilo is one of his most recent architecture projects.

The Suppanen house is on its own island, which takes about 20 minutes to reach by boat from the nearest inhabited island. It could be described as a typical Finnish summerhouse when it comes to its appliances and equipment, in that it has neither running water nor an electric cable to the mainland. The electricity supply is created by a system of solar panels. Instead, the house is self-sufficient and reliant on what the natural world around it can provide. When asked whether the house is typically Finnish, the architect Ilkka Suppanen simply answers, 'The house is in the middle of nature and, once you are there, you

OPPOSITE The pine ceiling curves around the whole house, sucking in the chimney tops from the kitchen and fireplace. The kitchen is nothing out of the ordinary; haute cuisine is not a priority among Finnish country house owners.

ABOVE The Suppanen house is a real rural retreat, located as it is far away from neighbours and any signs of urban life. Yet the architect behind it has created a contemporary haven in the middle of the Baltic Sea. In true Finnish tradition, the surrounding woods are both outside and inside – serving as a constant reminder of where you are.

LEFT The fireplace with its concrete bench projecting left from the roaring fire is one of the best features of the house, especially in winter. It was built by the present owners, and is extremely heavy. Note the simple, functional firewood basket.

are part of nature. But is this really Finnish? I do not really think of this once I am designing something.'

Set on the highest point of the island, the building has a curved form that follows the contour of the rocky landscape. The ideal location for the villa was precisely calculated; it is oriented to take advantage of the sun's path and nature's diurnal rhythm. The site needed to offer protection from the prevailing Baltic winds, since the weather in this area can be fierce all year round. The house offers wonderful sea views and has plenty of attractive rock formations nearby, which is typical of the Åland archipelago. The potential difficulties presented by a site in such a steep spot were evident to Suppanen, but he felt that these only served to add to the dramatic qualities of the house.

The house's area is 85 sq m (102 sq yd) and its sauna covers a further 25 sq m (30 sq yd). Proportionately, this might seem like a generous allocation of space for the sauna, but it is perfectly normal for a Finnish house. Indeed, a Finnish country house without a sauna is considered not only poor but bordering on the suspect. The choice is between an electric sauna (common in the city) and a traditional wood-fired sauna, like the one installed here. The effect of an electric sauna is deemed to be completely different from that of a wood-fired sauna; the latter is more intense. The sauna is situated on a flat area near the tip of a headland, where it is exposed to winds nearly all the time. To minimize erosion, a large terrace has been laid around the sauna building. The dressing room, washroom and sauna itself are separated by glass partitions to create the feeling of there being just one simple space. Steam generated by bathing in the sauna and washing steams up the glass partitions and provides privacy.

The choice of pine as the building material is, in the words of the architect, 'a very practical solution' – a comment that exemplifies the Finnish attitude not only to building but also to life in general. This intensely practical approach does not stop there. The house was built by just two men, the father and son who planned to live there, so it was crucial that none of the construction elements exceeded the maximum weight that could be carried by two people.

It took some effort to acquire building permission. The authorities were concerned that the house would be visible from the sea, so Suppanen experimented with various alternatives and produced a large number of drawings to convince them that this would not be a problem. A local contractor built the kitchen to Suppanen's brief, while the father and son owners constructed the fireplace. The bench was also built by the owners to Suppanen's design; it is made of concrete and covered by black glass plates. The interior is peppered with Finnish design classics: Alvar Aalto tables, stools and chairs by Artek, the Harri Koskinen K chair for Woodnotes and traditional firewood baskets.

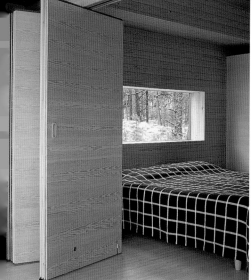

The ideal location of the villa was precisely calculated; it is oriented to take advantage of the sun's path and nature's diurnal rhythm.

THIS PAGE, INSET AND RIGHT The sleeping section can be closed off by a large, sliding door fixed to a wooden beam in the ceiling. The bed area is close to one of the fireplaces, making it warm and comfortable. Visible just outside – like a snapshot of nature – is the untamed pine forest. The benches by the foot of the bed are by Alvar Aalto for Artek.
OPPOSITE The woven firewood basket made of birch can be found in farmers' markets across the country.

genius
in glass

When Ingegerd Råman and her partner Claes bought their house on Österlen in the southern Swedish province of Skåne, it was essentially an untouched 1920s school building. Little of the original floor plan with its two large teaching rooms has been changed, except for the removal of some internal doors and partitions. All of the original floorboards were kept, even though a great deal of love and attention was required to restore them to their former glory.

Claes did most of the building work himself and acted as a self-appointed site foreman. The entire job was completed in only four months. This included the painstaking renovation of the large windows; both of the owners were determined not to replace them with modern copies in suspect materials.

The collaboration with the young but successful architectural trio of Mårten Claesson, Eero Koivisto and Ola Rune was crucial to the success of the project. In Sweden,

OPPOSITE The installation of the sliding-glass wall was one of the few alterations made to the old school house. **ABOVE RIGHT** The long dining table is a design by Claesson Koivisto Rune to the owners' specifications. The chairs are heirlooms, that nicely complement the strict table design. **BELOW RIGHT** The fireplace in the corner is a Swedish tile stove, famous for its superior heat distribution. This one was made in Karlskrona in 1925, but was put in by Ingegerd and Claes. The chaise longue is by Källemo.

THIS PAGE The daybed, made to the owners' design, is there for the comfort of anyone who wants to have a little rest while the other is busy in the adjoining kitchen. The floor lamp is a 1958 design by Arne Jacobsen. The floorboards are the originals and date back to 1925 when the building was constructed for use as a schoolhouse. **OPPOSITE** The desk, whose inlaid-leather top is new, came from an old Swedish castle. The chair was picked up at an auction house.

Designer Ingegerd Råman's Swedish house is a study in contemporary minimalism.

Ingegerd Råman is the queen of modern, uncompromising, simple glass, while the architects are the champions of minimalist architecture and furniture design. They all share a passion for Japanese aesthetics and the limited colour palette of black and white; the architects are even described as the 'Men in Black', while she is rarely seen in any other colour.

Even in her early work in the 1960s, Råman turned against waves of colours and wild patterns. 'My work has always represented a link between simplicity, function and aesthetic values,' she says. In 1995, she was made Professor of Honour by the Swedish government, and was awarded the Prince Eugen

LEFT Ingegerd and Claes
designed the bed. The
long sideboard is by
Claesson Koivisto Rune.
The light is the classic
British Bestlite from the
1930s. In front of the bed
is a Japanese-inspired
installation that suits the
room's pared-back look.

Medal by the King of Sweden in 1998. One of her recent
commissions was for a new heraldic symbol of the Kingdom
of Sweden for the Swedish parliament, placed behind the
Speaker of the House. She has made stainless-steel cutlery
for the Swedish company Gense, and ceramics for the
Norwegian company Figgjo and Sweden's Gustavsberg.

Just beside the old house stands a modern white cube,
5 m (16 ft 4 in) high and with a slanted roof, which was
designed by Claesson Koivisto Rune. This is Ingegerd
Råman's ceramics studio. Råman does not particularly like
to be referred to by the title 'designer' – even though she is
a brilliant one – and prefers to be called a 'ceramicist', since
ceramics involves working with your hands. She creates

things by pushing the materials that she works with to the
limit. This has included the rediscovery of 1920s and 1930s
techniques of etching, but using totally modern patterns.
She experiments by marking the glass with grinders and
files, and consults glass-blowers about what can be done.

Although she trained as a ceramicist, it is through her
work in glass that Råman has attained commercial success
and fame. She first worked for the small but old and well-
respected Johansfors and Skruf glassworks in the 'glass
country' of Småland in southern Sweden, a couple of hours
away from her present country home. At Skruf, she made
official glassware for the Swedish parliament, the foreign
office and several Swedish embassies. She joined Orrefors,

the most revered of the Swedish glassworks, in 1999. There she has created, and continues to create, a succession of simple but exquisite bowls, vases and glasses. Her work is represented in numerous international museum collections and has been shown in many exhibitions both in Sweden and abroad.

The country house in Skåne is a clear extension of her and Claes's aesthetics. Many of the pieces – not that there are very many – are what you would expect in a trendy Scandinavian house: some Aalto, some Jacobsen, some Kjærholm. But when you speak to Ingegerd, she says, 'The Alvar Aalto bar stools – yes, we bought them in the late 1960s. The Jacobsen Ant chair – I think Claes brought that with him

when we met.' It is the same with her work. Some have criticized her for following trends, but her work has been as it is now for years. At the same time, Ingegerd knows which glass designers she likes and says so. Perhaps surprisingly, she likes Per Sundberg, even though he brought something of punk rock design into traditional Swedish glass.

Beside Ingegerd and Claes's bed is Äpplet (the Apple vase) by Ingeborg Lundin, an icon of Swedish glass design from Orrefors, shaped like the Beatles' apple but made a decade before the Fab Four adopted the symbol. Äpplet is one of the most sought-after and collectable of all Swedish glass designs – Ingegerd's work excluded of course.

ABOVE The all-concealing white kitchen is by Saari, a small Finnish kitchen company popular among modern Swedish architects. The bar stools, by Alvar Aalto, were bought by Ingegerd in the 1960s. **LEFT** On the kitchen work surface is some of Ingegerd Råman's latest works in etched black glass for Orrefors.

raw luxury

The Lauf family has four members: fashion designer Naja, husband John Allan, son Albert – and the sea, which stretches beyond this beachside house. 'We live with the sea in mind all the time, and take a swim every morning – even in the middle of winter!' says Naja.

The interior of the house is also inspired by the sea, but not in the usual naval themes of stripes and seashell motifs. Instead, the original floorboards have been left slightly rough like the decking of a ship, while the wooden furniture is as tactile as driftwood smoothed by the wind and the sea.

The colour scheme is cool and pared back, with white walls mirroring the sandy beach outside. Most of the beautiful large windows in this 1890s house have been left without curtains or blinds, to give unrestricted views of the glittering expanse of water outside.

When the family moved in 16 years ago, the house was in a bad condition and they had to start from scratch with the interior. 'We had to strip an awful lot of wallpaper, take down a few walls to create the open-plan space we have now and build a completely new kitchen,' says Naja.

ABOVE It's summer all year round in this light, airy house by the sea north of Copenhagen. The glossy painted floorboards reflect back any ray of sunlight that sneaks through the windows, and the poster from the Bellevue beach lends a happy, retro feel. Stripes and rattan hint at the maritime setting outside the window.

THIS PAGE The Arne
Jacobsen table and chairs
look perfect in this airy
setting, while the light is an
early Poul Henningsen. The
cabinet was found on the
beach, and is an old safety
box used by swimmers to
deposit their valuables.

THIS PAGE Floaty curtains stir every time the wind blows, creating motion in the room and bringing the elements in. The rattan chairs are from Ikea and are teamed with stripey cushions.

But some original features were too beautiful to be scrapped, like the unusually large bathroom and the lovely windows.

The dining area faces out towards the sea, so the family can look out over the water while they eat. The chairs and table are by Arne Jacobsen, and Naja has a love of design classics without falling for ostentatious statement pieces: 'I grew up with items like the Papa Bear chair by Hans Wegner, so it's natural for me. For example, the light above the table is by Poul Henningsen, but came much earlier than his more famous PH lamp.'

The unusual pale-wood cabinet hides much of the family's clutter and was a true find. 'We picked it up on the beach,' says Naja. 'It was used as a safety box where visitors could put their valuables when they went for a swim, and when it wasn't needed any more we felt we could give it a good home.'

On top of the cabinet is a painting by Naja's father, Otto Lauf, and an assortment of binoculars. 'There is so much activity on the stretch of water outside, with ships going between Sweden and Denmark, sailing yachts and motorboats – we are really curious, so spend a lot of time checking out what's going on with the binoculars!' laughs Naja.

The olive tree next to the cabinet might well be Mediterranean, but it sits well in this northern seascape. 'This house does feel like a summerhouse,' says Naja, 'and that's fine by us, as it's our favourite season.'

The sea-facing windows in the living room are beautiful enough to become displays in their own right – the striped pattern of the radiator draws the eye to the symmetry of the windows, while the delicate flower and painting prevent the space from becoming too austere.

The living room is also stripped back and conveys a feeling of calm. The large sofa is from Italian company Arketipo, while the coffee table was skilfully made out of a large piece of elm tree by Naja's husband, John Allan. He has the

ABOVE The family likes big, comfy sofas, like this one from Italian company Arketipo, topped with plump cushions. The coffee table was made by Anja's husband, while the simple white flowers are reminiscent of the beach plants outside.

ABOVE In the bedroom, pattern has been created through unusual means — the vintage radiator, with its strict ridges and sharp lines, is complemented by the stripey cushions on the bed. The black reading light perches comfortably on top, and draws the eye towards it along the radiator lines. The strictness of the scheme is toned down by the sky-blue cushion with circular patterns on the bed and the delicate vase of flowers beside it. A simple white stool serves as a little table. The white cotton duvet cover adds to the feeling of light and space in this room.

enviable position of living right on top of his place of work — beach inspector for north Copenhagen, where the house is located.

The cane chairs were bought at Ikea, and are topped with stripey cushions from Day Birger et Mikkelsen. The walls are left bare so as to reflect as much light as possible. They are painted in a soft white, the sole, timeless adornment being a beautifully wrought cover for a heating outlet.

A group of old fishing rods nestles in the corner. 'We only bought them because of their beauty,' says Naja. 'They were from an old lady who had been widowed, and didn't know what to do with her husband's old rods. We were happy to give them a new lease of life.'

At the back of the house runs a terrace that overlooks the Øresund strait, the stretch of water dividing Denmark from Sweden. This is where Naja grows her plants and entertains — there is room for eight at the table and the terrace is perfect for whiling away long summer evenings and watching the sun set over the sea.

The family can even cook out here using the outdoor kitchen. 'The weather here is normally

ABOVE LEFT Day Birger et Mikkelsen's home line is one of the most successful in Denmark, due in part to their ability to take traditional patterns and make them look modern. **ABOVE CENTRE** The little heart-shaped stone was a gift to Naja from her young son, Albert. **ABOVE RIGHT** Simple blooms and flowers look right at home in this house. **BELOW** Carefully arranged items on a paint-flecked stool make an elegant still life.

very good, even when it's not great inland,' says Naja. 'We cook here as much as we possibly can in the summer, apart from when the wind blows in hard from the sea.' Dinner is always eaten by the light of an old storm lantern, which emits just enough light during the long Scandinavian summer evenings when the sun takes forever to disappear.

A piece of driftwood has been turned into a hook for a jug, which comes in handy for the cold-water tap/faucet outside. But the rustic way of life doesn't quite stretch to doing the washing up outside, using cold water. 'No, we leave that to the dishwasher inside,' smiles Naja.

The charming bathroom is unusually large for such an old house and the original bathtub and wall tiles have been kept. 'This is my favourite room in the house,' says Naja. It has such a calm feeling to it, with hints of retro such as the old shaving mirror and the jug on the radiator. Having little personal items scattered round, like Kaj Bojesen's wooden elephant and the statue on the shelf, ensures that the space remains cozy and stops it feeling too much like a communal

swimming pool. The walls are painted white, like the rest of the house.

The pared-back design scheme continues in the bedroom. Here, Naja has once again made use of the radiators to create a pattern in the room, rather than hiding them away behind a wooden cover. The symmetrical pattern of the heater is mirrored in the cushions on the bed, while the angular light breaks the rigidity. The circular shape of the castors appears again in the round lamp above the bed, showing perfectly how pattern and interest can be created in a room without over-decorating it — a very Scandinavian way of looking at beauty.

And this beautiful house, nestling between two Nordic countries, with its love of light, good design and natural materials, is just about as Scandinavian as they come.

OPPOSITE A terrace runs outside the dining area with stunning sea views. **ABOVE LEFT AND RIGHT** In the summertime the family and guests spend as much time gazing out over the water as possible. The outdoor furniture is simple but rustic, and can withstand the rough weather of the Øresund region. There is an outdoor sink with running water where dishes can be rinsed off, so as not to miss any valuable time alfresco. The storm lantern spreads just enough light when the sun starts dipping below the horizon, and won't sputter and die out with the wind. A weathered piece of driftwood has been turned into a hook on the wall.

designer home

Mikko Puotila runs Woodnotes, a company he set up with his mother, the Finnish textile designer Ritva Puotila. Her large-scale textile artworks can be seen in many institutions and corporate headquarters both in Finland and abroad. Ritva Puotila first began experimenting with wood fibre as a textile material in the 1960s, and in the late 1980s she and Mikko Puotila took the bold decision to establish a company producing items made from the material.

When Ritva and Mikko Puotila set up their company, wood fibre was a deeply unfashionable, utilitarian material, associated with hard times. Wood fibre had been used in Finland to replace imported cotton in wartime, and was also used to insulate underground telephone cables. The Puotilas managed to purchase the last factory in Finland specializing

ABOVE LEFT The kitchen has a sea view, but the main work surface overlooks the living room. Black Series 7 chairs and an Eero Saarinen Tulip table with an Italian Arabescato marble top are used for informal meals.
ABOVE RIGHT With simple crockery and a Woodnotes runner, the table setting has an oriental flavour. The tall console table offers display space, but also keeps treasures out of the reach of tiny fingers. The cube bookshelves were custom-made.

THIS PAGE The large Kuutti Lavonen painting is entitled Regina Celi. Stacked on the floor are two large cushions from the Woodnotes collection. Outside, the balcony runs the whole length of the living room.

in wood-fibre insulated cables, and converted the 30-year-old machinery to make wood-fibre rugs. Woodnotes is now a successful company that exports the majority of its products. It produces blinds, rugs, furniture, room dividers, placemats, table runners and a collection of handbags – all crafted from humble wood fibre.

When Mikko Puotila, together with his girlfriend and newborn baby son, moved into a building in Espoo, near Helsinki, they called on interior architect Ulla Koskinen for advice. Although the building, which dated from 1981, was designed by the well-known architects Gullichsen-Kairamo-Vormala, the floor plan of their new apartment needed a radical rethink. The flat consisted of several small rooms and a long, narrow kitchen. Mikko Puotila wanted to transform it into an open space generously lit with natural daylight and with uninterrupted views of the sea.

Ulla Koskinen came up with the idea of relocating the kitchen in a former bedroom with an en suite bathroom,

THIS PAGE Sliding doors lead to the master bedroom, which was created by removing a wall between two smaller rooms. The modular sofa is by B&B Italia.
OPPOSITE BELOW Like so many Finnish homes, this one has its own sauna. More than just a hot room for cleansing the body, the sauna is used for relaxation and social gatherings, with cold drinks close to hand.

ABOVE LEFT An orchid adds a splash of the exotic to this tranquil living space. **ABOVE CENTRE LEFT** The simple colour scheme of the room is mirrored in these comfortable cushions. **ABOVE CENTRE RIGHT** A collection of miniature vases in earthy tones looks right at home on top of the wood-pannelled bathtub.

ABOVE RIGHT A room with a view – the bathroom looks out over the Baltic Sea. The floor and walls are clad in marble tiles and a sandblasted glass screen acts as a room divider, adding to the feeling of light in this room. The bathtub is encased with wenge wood and the sleek Vola tap/faucet is designed by Arne Jacobsen.

which meant that the existing plumbing could be utilized. Instead of positioning the kitchen work surfaces against an outside wall, the kitchen was opened up towards the living room. The wall between two small bedrooms was removed to create one large master bedroom. All the internal doors were replaced or simply taken out, and some of the doorways were widened, to increase the feeling of space. Skirting boards were removed before an oiled oak floor was laid. Puotila's young son now has plenty of uninterrupted floor space to play and crawl on.

Mikko Puotila has furnished his home with a number of Scandinavian design classics, including Arne Jacobsen's Series 7 chairs and Vola taps/faucets, and an Eero Saarinen table, teamed with several modern Italian designs and a selection of pieces from Woodnotes, including oversized floor cushions, rugs and seating cubes. The only Woodnotes products used sparingly are their blinds – the views of the Baltic Sea outside are just too good to hide.

Contemporary Rustic

Tradition and the way people used to live weighs heavily on Scandinavian designers' shoulders, but this doesn't stop them putting a modern twist on old methods and creating a whole new design language. This is mainly done through materials. Wood is constantly being reinvented, from the discovery of how to produce bentwood to creating whole kitchens out of chipboard and flat-packing them. Stone is reshaped to make sleek surrounds for bathtubs and fireplaces, and skins and hides are casually thrown over stylish chairs to create a warm ambience. This rustic style is kept fresh by the clean lines of the furniture within it — any other way and the scheme is instantly heavy and outdated.

modern natural

This Norwegian home is located on an island in Vestfold, on the western side of the Oslo fjord, the nearest larger town being Tønsberg. This is an area that has been colonized by summer visitors from Oslo since the early 20th century, and the population now increases almost tenfold during the summer. The district has a rich wildlife, including many species of seabird, elk, deer and even lynx. Mink can sometimes be seen on the smaller islands furthest out to sea. The southern point of Tjøme island is known as Verdens Ende – the World's End – and looks out onto the open sea.

The house was built in 2003 and designed by the architects Lund Hagem, a relatively large firm headed by Suein Lund and Einar Hagem,

ABOVE LEFT The low bench along the front of the fireplace is made of concrete. The large artwork above the mantel is by Norwegian artist Geis Harald Samuelsen and is made from sheets of lead sprayed with high-gloss automotive paint. **BELOW LEFT** The sofa and coffee table were both made for the house, while the easy chairs are from Ikea. The furniture, like the floor, is made from aspen; walls and ceilings are ash.

THIS PAGE The dining table, sofa and bookshelves are all built in ash and made specially for the house. Simple teak chairs like those used in the courtyard are also used for dining. The small pendant lights are from the Danish company Herstal. A slanted skylight illuminates the dining area and kitchen.

LEFT The kitchen units are custom-made, like all the other fixed furniture in the house, while the kitchen appliances are from Miele. Instead of large overhanging cabinets, a free-hanging shelf was installed so that the kitchen area would retain its light appearance.
OPPOSITE ABOVE The kitchen work surface is made of concrete, like many other parts of the house. Most of the glass items above it are by Benny Motzfeldt, who was a pioneer in Norwegian glass design. She worked for Christiania Glassmagasin, Hadeland and Randsfjord glassworks, and the Plus glass studio in Fredrikstad.

among whose many projects is a country house for the King of Norway. Designed to provide shelter from the wind, this house opens up towards a courtyard at the centre. The idea was to use as few materials and colours as possible to give the house a calm and unified appearance. The three main materials are concrete, aspen and ash wood, with a colour palette of greys and natural wood.

The area between the house and the open sea is a nature reserve, which the public are free to visit but not to build on.

In Norway, as in many other countries, building is prohibited along the coast in order to protect it for future generations. But the seafront can be enjoyed in many other ways. The family who lives in this house keeps both a small motorboat for fishing and two kayaks that are used frequently to explore the neighbouring islands and skerries.

Most of the furniture in the house has been specially made for this location, and fixed to the wall to create the impression that it is part of the structure and to keep loose

BELOW The wooden floor in the bathroom is laid with gaps between the floorboards so that water can run between them and out of the hole in the concrete beneath. The floor planks are loose so that they can be removed for cleaning underneath – the practical element of the house's design is ever present.

items to a minimum. The ash used for the bespoke furniture matches the ash of the floor, bringing the two together. The ash bookshelves are integrated with the walls rather than freestanding so as to add to the feeling of space. It requires a certain discipline to keep the house free of clutter, but the owners have succeeded in doing this.

The family tends to use the house in Vestfold mainly during the summer months. Norwegians are very enthusiastic about outdoor sports and exercise, perhaps even more so than their Scandinavian neighbours. The family likes to ski and in winter they usually stay in a cabin in the mountains further north, close to the ski slopes. They like to visit their coastal country home around Christmas though.

Natural vegetation growing near the building has been left pretty much to its own devices. A small area near the house has been covered with sand for ball games, and there are wild rose bushes and juniper bushes growing nearby. The courtyard has a vine-covered wall that produces grapes each summer.

The concrete-covered courtyard is framed by a sunken strip filled with round stones of various sizes that have been collected from the area by the owners. This is an endless project, since each walk along the beach or meadow might bring up another decorative stone, shaped by nature over the years. The dining table in the courtyard is also made from concrete, while the outdoor dining chairs are of the same type as used around the indoor dining table. The courtyard has a shower with a large head that proves handy as an extra facility during the summer months.

The wooden flooring in the bathroom has been laid with gaps between the boards so that splashed water is able to run between them.

ABOVE TOP The desk looks straight out onto a large expanse of vegetation – you couldn't find a more tranquil place to think and work. **ABOVE BELOW** The concrete is framed by a sunken strip filled with round stones collected from the area by the owners, each chosen for its special appeal.

OPPOSITE The courtyard shower is a useful facility. When the weather is clement, it is preferred to its counterpart outdoors. **ABOVE RIGHT** Natural vegetation, including wild roses and juniper bushes, has been allowed to encroach on the building, and there is a nature reserve nearby. **CENTRE RIGHT** Concrete is the material used to make the dining table in the courtyard. The outdoor chairs are of the same type as those used for dining indoors. **BELOW RIGHT** The courtyard is designed to be protected from the wind, making it the perfect spot for outdoor entertaining, even on gustier days. One wall is covered with a grapevine that gives fruit each summer.

Underneath is a concrete screed with a hole for the water to run out of, and underfloor heating; the floor planks are loose so that they can easily be removed for cleaning underneath. This creates a perfectly functional floor, while allowing the wood featured in the rest of the house to also be used in the bathroom. The concrete frame that the bathtub sits in continues out through the window by the end of the tub to become an outdoor bench, so that there is a sense of the indoor and outdoor coming together while you are taking a bath.

The house in Vestfold was recently featured in an exhibition curated by the National Museum in Oslo as one of the 10 best buildings to be constructed in Norway over the past few years (50 buildings in total). Corporate, public and private buildings were included in the exhibition, but only two country houses. One of them was an addition to an existing structure, while the other was this house. It just goes to show that less can certainly end up being more when it comes to new builds.

understated
comfort

The country house of Elina Helenius and her partner Mika Mahlberg stands right on the beach of the largest lake in southern Finland, Lake Lohja. It was designed by the acclaimed Finnish architect Matti Sanaksenaho and completed in 2002. Built over one floor, the house occupies a total area of about 65 sq m (78 sq yd).

The plot on which the house was built is next door to land owned by Elina Helenius's parents. It is quite common in Finland to divide up land so that space is made available to build a country house for the younger generation. In many cases, the land will have been acquired many years earlier, when prices were more affordable, and having your children as neighbours means that you really are familiar with the people on your doorstep.

It makes perfect sense if two generations living next door to each other share a sauna house between them, as is the case here. Finland, a nation of 5 million people, has some 1.5 million saunas. Both men and women bathe in the sauna, but never together, except within the family. When friends are invited for a sauna, it is customary to agree who goes first, men or women. Often the women are invited to go first, out of courtesy, or if they are in charge of preparing the dinner afterwards.

Finland has the highest proportion of second-home ownership in Europe – some 25 per cent of Finns own a

second home – but it is not a symbol of wealth as in other countries. Owning a second home has more to do with there being a strong culture of spending time in the countryside and the fact that large parts of Finland are thinly populated, so it is still affordable to buy land or country homes. The situation is different in the Helsinki region, however as more people are moving to the area and so prices are increasing. The archipelago and coast are also very popular.

The Helenius family use their country home all year round, but their longest stay is in the summer, often for six weeks. Like most Finns, they deliberately live a simple but comfortable life while there, without television. They tend to live mainly on fresh fish from Lake Lohja and rye bread.

In summer the windows are left free of blinds or curtains to let in as much light as possible. Doors are kept wide open, so that nature is only a step away. Finland is one of the safest and least crime-ridden countries in the world, and locking the door is the exception rather than the rule in country homes. Textiles are more evident in winter, when a warmer feeling is required; curtains are hung up and throws are put out for bundling oneself up in.

Elina Helenius designed the interior of the house herself, a task for which she is more than well qualified. She started her design career at the Finnish textile company Marimekko in 1989 and stayed there until 1992. She had previously been a teacher of print design at Lahti Polytechnic and has been a

OPPOSITE The cushion cover is by Elina Helenius and the low bench by Mika Mahlberg. The ceramic lamp foot is an old design from Arabia in Helsinki. LEFT A pair of chairs by James Irvine for Ikea. Sheepskins formerly used on the children's sledges have found a new use. The cushion covers are Helenius's design. BELOW RIGHT The fireplace and staircase are made of slate from Orivesi, southern Finland. The floor lamp is a prototype designed by Petri Vainio for Doctor Design, a Helsinki-based company for which Helenius also works.

lines and colours of the pale wood to remain visible and is highly decorative. It is typical of Sanaksenaho's architecture – natural wood is a theme that he keeps returning to, and it is also very Finnish; Finland is the biggest timber nation in Scandinavia. The only contrasting material is the dark Finnish slate that has been used for the fireplace and that spills over onto the floor and staircase around it. The light grout is a stark contrast to the dark stone and emphasizes the irregular pieces of slate.

To make the most of the space, there is a raised sleeping alcove with storage underneath. Sliding doors close it off from the rest of the house, ensuring that the sleepers get privacy. There is an obvious Japanese influence in the design. The kitchen has a very simple look, as befits a Finnish country house. It has open shelves above the work surface holding glass and crockery; mainly old and new Arabia ceramics. Instead of a splashback, Sanaksenaho has placed two long, narrow windows above the work surface; wherever you are in the house, you're never far from an amazing view of the natural world outside.

lecturer at the University of Art and Design in Helsinki since 2003. She has also worked as a textile designer for the Finnish company Doctor Design since 2002. Many of her textile designs are used in this house.

Matti Sanaksenaho, the house's architect, studied at the Helsinki University of Technology. He has been a visiting professor at Aarhus Arkitektskole in Denmark and taught architecture at the University of Technology. One of his most publicized projects was the St Henry's Ecumenical Art Chapel in Turku, built in 2005. It is a fantastic wooden church building that resembles an upturned boat.

The floor of the house is clear-lacquered pine, while the walls are made from conifer veneer. This allows the grain

moving lodge

THIS PAGE & OPPOSITE Beside the fireplace is a Code firewood basket made from white-lacquered steel by Ola Vihlborg for Asplund. The cubes in front of it are by Katrin Hefter. The armchairs, called Box, are by Piero Lissoni for Living Divani. Both seating options mirror the rigid lines of the fireplace, which provides a focal point, particularly during the cold winter months.

The original purpose of the Vistet house was to demonstrate how 18th-century building techniques could be regarded as environmentally friendly and energy efficient at the end of the 20th century. The project required two skilled architects and a team of equally skilled timber builders. Once completed, the house was put on show in 1997 in the Swedish city of Kalmar during the 600th jubilee of the 1397 Kalmar Union, a political agreement that united Scandinavia. The house was then moved to Stockholm in time for the 1998 European Capital of Culture celebrations. It was placed outside the entrance of Nordiska Museet (the Nordic Museum), the national Swedish museum for culture after 1520, and opened to the public from February to December 1998.

Finally, the Vistet house was put up for auction and bought by Nils Tunebjer and his

THIS PAGE & OPPOSITE BELOW Some of the most renowned Swedish designers collaborated on the original interior of the Vistet house when it was exhibited. Owner Nils Tunebjer has picked out the best of the best. The dining table is by Johan Edjemo for Asplund, with a pendant light above it by Katrin Hefter; the dining chairs are by John Kandell for Källemo. The dotted rug is by Pia Wallén for Asplund, while the interlocking stools, called wedding stools, are by Thomas Sandell for Asplund.

family. Tunebjer did not have a plot of land to put the house on; indeed, he had had no intention of bidding at the auction. But when the bidding was slow, he was tempted, and ended up owning a unique house. What made the house even more interesting for him was that, while two well-known architects had designed it in a modern style, its timber construction followed old Swedish building technology, with interlocking beam-ends and internally visible trunks of timber.

The Vistet architect Thomas Sandell, together with Gert Wingårdh and the trio Claesson Koivisto Rune, are among the best-known Swedish architects today. A former president of SAR, the National Association of Swedish Architects, Sandell taught architecture to Victoria, the Crown Princess of Sweden. As a furniture designer, he has collaborated with several Swedish and foreign furniture producers: Artek, Asplund, B&B Italia, Cappellini, CBI, Gärsnäs, Ikea, Källemo, Mobileffe and Tronconi. His interiors include the Stockholm stock exchange, the Wallpaper House in Milan in 1999, the restaurant at the Museum of Modern Art in Stockholm, the Ericsson office in London and several notable Stockholm restaurants such as East and Rolfs Kök; the latter is now a listed interior.

Thomas Sandell's style has repeatedly been described as typically Swedish (even though he is originally from Finland), and he has often been held up as a flag carrier of the connection

RIGHT The cubic theme of the room is picked up again in the vertical bookshelf – a Swedish classic from 1989 called the Pilaster by John Kandell for Källemo. The freestanding lamp is also by Katrin Hefter for the now-defunct Swedish furniture company CBI.

between the old and the new in Swedish design. This may be reading too much into his work, however; he is essentially a modern designer.

The other Vistet architect, Anders Landström, specializes in timber construction, a skill gained during his childhood in northern Sweden, where it has been the norm since houses were first built hundreds of years ago. Apart from private homes, he is also responsible for the Swedish Embassy in Pretoria, South Africa, and the repair of many older buildings. With regard to Vistet, he points out how well a traditional timber construction keeps dry inside and how suitable it is for people with allergies, since it incorporates nothing but natural materials. While concrete might be easier to shape, timber is a very economical material, both environmentally and in monetary terms. Even in Scandinavia, this is a fact worth repeating.

After he had bought the Vistet house, the first problem for Nils Tunebjer was where to store it until he found somewhere to put it up. Luckily, the house came with its own carpenter, who had helped to build it and who now had the task of taking it apart piece by piece.

While trying to decide where to erect the house, Tunebjer thought of the outer south Stockholm archipelago, whose pebbled beaches, pine trees, cliffs and austere landscape would make a good setting for the building. He bought a plot of land on a remote island and had the house rebuilt. He also asked

ABOVE A mobile designed by Alexander Calder, from the Danish company Flensted, hangs from the ceiling of the guest house.

LEFT The painting of a bird adds a flamboyant touch to an otherwise pared-down bathroom. The little white wall tiling gives a neat effect, while the nifty, compact design of the toilet adds to the feeling of space.

Anders Landström to design two smaller, matching guesthouses, placed at a 90-degree angle to the main house so as to resemble an old farmstead. The house was already fitted with a solid-wood kitchen designed by Sandell, with a work surface made from cast iron treated against rust. Landström designed a fireplace that is the focal point of the main living area, while the creature comforts of electricity, plumbing and hot water were also installed.

The Tunebjer family uses the house all year round, even during the tough Scandinavian winters. The island where the house stands is so far out into the Baltic that the open waters around it never freeze. Instead, ice flakes are pushed onto the island and stack up on the beach by the house, sometimes creating piles up to 3 m (10 ft) tall. The winds and waves are strong around the island; it is one of the few places in Sweden where you can surf. But the thick timber construction keeps the house as warm inside as any modern insulation material, and the raw timber roof has not required any maintenance since it was built. 'It's a matter of quality through and through,' says Tunebjer.

LEFT Modern yet traditional, the Vistet house relies on ancient construction techniques. It looks as if it has been in its location for more than a hundred years, despite being transported around Sweden for three years until 2000. In a way, it is the ultimate Swedish country house, but it is also a document of the present. Yet it is still a unique building that represents only itself and not the norm. The apparently randomly placed windows owe more to Le Corbusier than to ancient Swedish farmers, but the timber joints clearly have their origins in traditional Swedish house building. **BELOW** The present owner has discovered the right location for the house's ultimate resting place, yet it was not designed for any specific location. The outdoor dining area makes for a tranquil spot during the summer months.

house
on stilts

Aki Wahlman is well known in Finland through his magic in the kitchen. He was awarded Chef of the Year in 1996; he has made five different television series since then, and has worked for various restaurants in Finland and Sweden. Also a qualified teacher, he has taught at Turku University of Applied Sciences. He lives just outside Turku on the west coast of Finland when he is not at his country home.

The house is called Villa Nina and the sauna building Rosa-Maria. The buildings are set on a large island in the north Turku archipelago, in the Baltic Sea. The surrounding countryside is covered with birch and fir trees and slopes gently down towards the sea. In common with most other beaches in Finland, the shore is covered with bare rock. During autumn and winter, the faraway lighthouse at Isokari can be seen blinking on the horizon. There is a sturdy bridge by the water; the icy winters are known for taking with them any weak structures.

Rather than being set straight onto rocky ground, the house was mounted on steel and concrete pillars so that the impact on the ancient rocks below would be minimal. The

ABOVE This striking piece is a version of Alvar Aalto's tea trolley, originally designed for Artek in the 1930s.
OPPOSITE The Karuselli chair by Yrjö Kukkapuro for Avarte from 1964 is the focal point of the living area. Its design is based on the idea of throwing yourself into the deep Finnish snow and letting your body shape the imprint. The sculpture is a plaster model for a larger sculpture by Oiva Olavi Waittinen.

LEFT The house on stilts was designed by two architecture students, Kimmo Köpilä and Topi Laaksonen. It was built in two phases during 2004 and 2005. The large expanse of glass lets in maximum light and views of the nearby water. The decking is sheltered from the elements thanks to the projecting roof. **BELOW** The sauna building has a living room with a long, narrow window that gives views of the sea so that after a sauna you can take a look at the weather and decide to throw yourself into the water or simply have a shower. The easy chairs are from Ikea, but look distinctly Finnish in this setting. **OPPOSITE** The coffee table is custom-made by the design company NollaNolla, known for the interior of the trendy Helsinki restaurant Via. The wicker basket is made of willow. The rug is from Ikea. The light brown leather Wassily chairs by Marcel Breuer were designed in 1925 and are second-hand finds.

The house was mounted on steel pillars so that the impact on the ancient rocks below would be minimal.

THIS PAGE The kitchen units in walnut veneer are custom-made, as is the dining table. The dark-stained interior wall extends into the exterior, blurring the boundary between inside and outside with the snow-white dining chairs providing a contrast. While there are steps up to the kitchen, the ceiling height stays the same so that the living area at the back of the house is more intimate than at the front. The glass is inserted straight into the load-bearing frames; it has gas between the panes to supply thermal insulation.

ABOVE LEFT The delicate willow wicker basket contrasts beautifully with the rough, thick-piled rug that sits beneath the dining-room table. **ABOVE CENTRE** Suspended over the table are the famous Golden Bell brass pendant lights, designed by Alvar Aalto in the 1930s. The comfortable dining chairs are another Finnish design classic: the Kilta chair by Olli Mannermaa from 1955, recently put back into production by Martela. These particular chairs are originals that Wahlman had reupholstered. **ABOVE RIGHT** The dining table was especially made for the house and is strategically placed by the window so that diners can make the most of the wonderful views while they enjoy a meal cooked by the award-winning chef.

main building materials are wood and glass. The façade is made from black-stained pine constructed according to a technique borrowed from Norway. Laid horizontally, it has open joints between the boards to allow air to circulate. The large glass surfaces are made from thick glass inserted straight into the load-bearing frames. The double-glazing consists of two 6-mm (¼-in) panes enclosing a gas that provides thermal insulation.

The main building is a rectangular U-shape, with the opening of the U facing inland, away from the wind. The living area is situated on the west, facing the setting sun, while the bedrooms are in their own wing on the eastern side. The roof is covered with untreated copper, and the same material has been used for gutters and water spouts. Over time, the roof and gutters will take on a green patina. The roof slopes towards the inner courtyard at the centre of the U-shape to drain away rain and snow. Seen from a distance, the building looks as though it has a flat roof.

Since the floor is lower at the back of the house than at the front, while the roof and inner ceiling remain at the same level, there is an apparent variation in ceiling height that puts the emphasis on the front room with its spectacular views to the horizon, where passing ships can be seen. Outside is a terrace covered by the projecting roof, which gives protection from rain and wind. On the side of the building is a semi-open atrium for use on summer evenings.

The kitchen units are made from walnut veneer. The Skandic tap/faucet in the kitchen and other similar appliances in the house are by the 175-year-old Swedish company Gustavsberg. The dining table was made especially for the house. The brass lights over the dining table are the famous Golden Bell pendants, designed by Alvar Aalto.

They were used both at Aalto's Savoy restaurant in Helsinki in 1937 and at his Poetry Room at Harvard University, USA, in 1948. The Golden Bell is no longer in production in this version, but Wahlman was lucky to find some made in the 1950s at a Helsinki café about to close down. The floor lights are also an Alvar Aalto design, called model A805 and designed by Aalto in 1953–54. They have a white-painted metal lampshade and a base and stand covered with black leather; the upper part is made of polished brass.

The dining chairs are comfortable enough to find a home in the bedroom as well. They are another Finnish design classic: the Kilta chair by Olli Mannermaa from 1955. In its time, the Kilta was sold in great numbers across the world, and is even represented in the permanent collection of the Museum of Modern Art in New York. Martela, the largest Finnish office furniture company, has recently started to

produce the chairs again. The Kilta chairs belonging to Aki Wahlman are original ones that he had reupholstered. They are used in several rooms.

The floor used throughout the inside of house is made from 120-mm (4¾-in) thick lacquered pine from Lapland in northern Finland. The pine has been coloured to match the larch that was used to cover the outdoor terrace floor. In the bedroom, the horizontal pine wall has been stained black, while the ceiling, also made of pine, has been treated with a light stain to create a contrast and make the ceiling seem higher. In the wood-fired sauna building, alder wood was chosen for the seating because it absorbs less heat than most other woods. Alder also gives off a natural scent when moist and warm. The sauna walls are treated with a moisture-resistant stain. Wahlman designed the interior of the house himself and approached every corner with care.

among
the trees

The forest home of architect Matti Sanaksenaho is an example of the very best of modern Finnish architecture. The house is located in Espoo, not far from Helsinki but far enough away to enjoy a wonderful surrounding forest and a view over the nearby lakes. Designed to bring the forest outside into the interior, the house is totally integrated into the landscape.

Sanaksenaho lives in the house with his family and has a small studio upstairs. Even though his home is a modest 150 sq m (180 sq yd) in size, there is nothing modest about Sanaksenaho's professional achievements. He was the man behind the highly acclaimed wood-clad Finnish pavilion at the World Exhibition in Seville in 1992 and was also responsible for creating the flagship store on the Esplanade in Helsinki for Designor, the company that owns Iittala, maker of the Aalto vases. Sanaksenaho also designed the Designor shop in Stockholm. Anyone who has seen these two stores would immediately recognize their similarities with Sanaksenaho's home, but this is not surprising, as Designor's brief was to make the stores look as though someone lived there.

ABOVE In the evening, the fireplace is the focus of the living room. It also helps to heat the house during the long, cold Finnish winter. **OPPOSITE** Triple glazing is now standard in most Finnish buildings, and makes building with large areas of glass perfectly viable, despite the cold winters.

The concept was not to build a grand mansion but to create a family home that would be completely integrated with the surrounding forest landscape. A terrace and a balcony add to the sense of space, while the large windows and expanses of glass bring the landscape in to the building. On warm days, meals and social gatherings are frequently enjoyed outside so as to take advantage of the fresh, pine-scented air and wonderful views.

The house was completed in 2002 and took about a year to build. The exterior is completely clad with Finnish pine, which was first heat-treated to ensure that it was completely dry and proof against any later warping or shrinkage. Pine is a good insulator that provides suitable protection against changing weather conditions, be they extreme heat or cold. Inside, the floor, parts of the ceiling and the gallery are crafted from birch, the classic Finnish wood. This type of wood reappears in the form of the birch furniture used throughout Sanaksenaho's home, much of which is designed by Alvar Aalto.

The house has triple glazing throughout – a standard Finnish domestic feature, along with having a sauna in the basement (another feature of this house). A heating system has been built into the ceiling of the 7-m (23-ft) high living room to project warmth downwards, and there are radiators built into the floor just inside the large windows. This very

TOP LEFT Sanaksenaho's home blends into its surroundings like a birdwatcher's hide. **TOP CENTRE** Finnish pines surround the Finnish-pine façade. The timber was heat-treated to ensure it was perfectly dry and provides good insulation against bad weather. **TOP RIGHT** The flat roof is tilted just enough to prevent snow from building up during the winter. The curved front makes reference to Aalto's Finlandia Hall, but on a domestic scale.

The curved façade of Sanaksenaho's house is certainly reminiscent of Finlandia Hall, Alvar Aalto's last large–scale building project Helsinki.

effective heating system has been teamed with a large fireplace for visual warmth and interest.

Sanaksenaho's home makes obvious references to the work of Alvar Aalto, but then Aalto himself was greatly influenced by the Finnish landscape, so it is unsurprising that anyone building a house in a Finnish forest would somehow refer to Aalto's organic style. The curved façade of Sanaksenaho's house is certainly reminiscent of Finlandia Hall, Aalto's last large-scale building project in Helsinki.

Sanaksenaho's house is very representative of modern Finnish architecture. It expresses a desire to bring the landscape indoors and to be close to nature, to enjoy plenty of natural daylight, yet be able to gather around a warm fire on dark winter nights. These needs and yearnings are deeply rooted in the Finnish psyche and hold the key to the beauty and integrity of Finnish architecture and design.

OPPOSITE The ceiling and gallery are clad with birch wood, the wood Alvar Aalto favoured for his furniture. In front of the bar stand two model K 65 kitchen stools designed by Aalto for Artek in 1933–35. The open-plan kitchen leads straight into the spacious living area.

ABOVE RIGHT The total ceiling height of the living room is an impressive 7 m (23 ft). In front of the birch-clad gallery hangs a PH 5 light by Poul Henningsen. **RIGHT** The zebra print chair adds a splash of pattern to the work area. It is a model 68 by Alvar Aalto, designed in 1933–35.

cabin fever

The west coast of Sweden has a landscape quite distinct from the greener Stockholm archipelago on the eastern side of Sweden, which is set in the Baltic Sea. The west coast faces straight onto the Atlantic and has a very different environment from that in the east, with different species of wildlife both above and below the water line.

People from the west coast of Sweden are quick to point out that they live at 'the front of Sweden', while the capital, Stockholm, is situated at 'the back'. There is a certain truth in this; the people of the west coast have relied for

ABOVE To underline the utilitarian look created by the large shutters, the wooden façade of the cabin has been stained silver-grey. The roof tiles are old and recycled, originally made in the 1920s. The outhouse is used for tools.

148

THIS PAGE The sofa below the window is by the Swede Bruno Mathsson and nestles perfectly below the long, narrow window.

many generations on seafaring and shipping, and it is much closer not only to Norway and Denmark but also to Britain and the Continent. Sweden's second largest city is Gothenburg, the capital of the west coast, sometimes referred to as Little London on account of its proximity to the British capital across the water. Besides shipping, the car manufacturer Volvo has its base at Gothenburg and has brought wealth to the region for many years.

Halland is the region starting just south of Gothenburg, stretching south along the coast until it reaches Skåne, like Halland itself a part of old Denmark. The main cities in Halland are Halmstad and Varberg, neither of them particularly large but both very popular in

summer. Halland is Sweden's prime golf region. Mild winters and early springs contribute to a long playing season, and within Halland's borders there are some 30 golf courses to keep people entertained.

It is no surprise, then, that the owner of this house in south-western Sweden is proud to have some 53 hectares (131 acres) of woodland, fields and islands along the popular coast of Halland. The estate includes an old farmstead and a 1930s stone house, but the architect Peter Hulting was called in to design three new buildings: the cabin, its matching outhouse and the main house, to be completed in 2007. At the moment, the cabin is used by the owners, but it will be turned into a guesthouse once the main

LEFT AND ABOVE The easy chair, like the dining chairs, is a design classic by Hans J. Wegner and makes for a peaceful resting spot by the window. The fireplace and floor are both made from concrete. Hidden out of sight behind the hanging textile is a sleeping area, complete with a wardrobe.

ABOVE The bathroom is one of the few rooms to be separated from the rest of the cabin by a door. The decor is kept pared back with simple white wall tiles and a small washbasin. LEFT The outhouse with its wall-mounted bench is visible through the bedroom window. It has been made exactly the same size as the cabin: 50 sq m (60 sq yd).

building is completed. The Atlantic Ocean is nearby, reaching up to the property through a shallow bay.

The cabin is very straightforward in its layout, consisting in essence of one long room with a high-pitched ceiling. The room combines all the functions; it is kitchen, dining room, sleeping area and living room all in one. Only the shower and WC are behind doors. The entire floor is covered in concrete that has deliberately been left unpolished. It still retains some of the roughness from when it was first put down, but has been clear-lacquered to stop it from giving off dust. The main material of the walls and ceiling is spruce, but the spruce has been mixed up with fir for a more uneven appearance.

The large window frames for the sliding doors are in lacquered steel, while the outside shutters are in Siberian larch. Hulting decided to put the sliding shutters outside rather than inside the windows for two reasons. First, it means that the windows can be open in summer while the shutters shield the interior from the heat, and second, the outside shutters make the cabin look more like an industrial shed than a pretty little country house. The exterior of the cabin has been stained silver-grey to reinforce the utilitarian look. The roof tiles are old and recycled, originally made in the 1920s.

The dining chairs and easy chair are by Hans J. Wegner, while the pendant over the dining table is an old PH5 by Poul Henningsen. The dining table is from Ikea and so are the stainless-steel fronts of the kitchen cupboards. The brightly coloured tiles behind the kitchen work surface are from Portugal. The sofa is by the Swedish architect and designer Bruno Mathsson. The chair in the bedroom is an old painted birch chair that has been stripped of its paint.

The cabin consists simply of one space that combines living area, dining room, kitchen and sleeping area.

RIGHT The Atlantic Ocean, in the form of a shallow bay, is just beyond the cliffs visible from the bedroom area. The deep window frames also serve as bookshelves; the edges were made to stick out into the room to give more surface. **BELOW** The open-plan living, dining and cooking areas sit together in perfect harmony, with the high ceilings adding to the feeling of space.

The structural stability of the house was put to a severe test by Gudrun, a storm with hurricane-force winds that hit Scandinavia in January 2005 while the owners were staying there. Across Scandinavia, 17 people were killed during the storm and another 10 during the clearing up. In Sweden, five nuclear reactors were shut down and all railway traffic was suspended. In southern Sweden, some 400,000 homes were deprived of electricity.

Gudrun felled 75 million cu m (98 cu yd) of forest in Sweden alone, almost equalling the country's annual felling total. The little cabin in Halland escaped relatively lightly, but the wind moved it by a small fraction, and the concrete floor cracked in places. The damage is still visible, but will soon be repaired. It took weeks before the cabin had its electricity supply restored, and the storm gave the owners a memory they will never forget.

sources

Arabia
www.arabia.fi
The company behind the beautiful range of Moomin mugs as well as other tableware items. Worldwide store locator available on website.

Artek
www.artek.fi
A modern design company based in Finland building on the heritage of Alvar Aalto. Stocks a wide range of Aalto designs with some products available through their online store.

Asplund
www.asplund.org
Specializing in high quality carpets and furniture. Online store locator.

Bestlite
www.bestlite.org.uk
This comprehensive website showcases the entire Bestlite collection and provides a list of dealers worldwide.

Cale Schiang Partnership
The Old Dairy
Tewin Hill Farm
Tewin Hill
Welwyn
Hertfordshire AL6 0LL
+44 (0)8702 202055
www.caleassociates.com
A wide selection of Hans Wegner and Bruno Mathsson furniture.

Cloudberry Living
www.cloudberryliving.co.uk
Online shop that carries designer gifts and home accessories from Scandinavia, from Moomin mugs to ferm LIVING cushions.

Co-existence
288 Upper Street
London N1 2TZ
+44 (0)20 7354 8817
www.coexistence.co.uk
Furniture by David Design and other Scandinavian designers.

The Conran Shop
www.conran.com
Arne Jacobsen and Verner Panton furniture and Le Klint lampshades.

Crate and Barrel/CB2
www.crateandbarrel.com
www.cb2.com
Crate and Barrel's designs with clean lines complement the Scandinavian look perfectly, as do CB2's, the cutting edge sister shop.

Danish Furniture Design
www.danishfurnituredesign.com
This company stocks vintage and modern furniture by all the leading design figures of Denmark such as Børge Mogensen and Verner Panton. Worldwide shipping available.

Day Birger et Mikkelsen
www.day.dk
This website showcases the label's fashion and homeware collections and has a worldwide store locator.

Design By Us
www.design-by-us.com
Based in Copenhagen, Design By Us is an interior design company.

Georg Jensen
www.georgjensen.com
Scandinavian silverware, including cutlery/flatware by Arne Jacobsen.

The Home
Salts Mill, Saltaire
Bradford BD18 3LB
+44 (0)1274 530770
www.thehomeonline.co.uk
A good selection of Scandinavian design, in particular Finnish design.

House of Fraser
Stores across the UK
www.houseoffraser.co.uk
Several House of Fraser stores stock Stelton kitchen and dining accessories.

Hygge
www.hyggelife.com
Online Danish shop filled with the coziest, most comfortable items for yourself and your home, from slippers to blankets. They also stock Kaj Bojesen's wooden toys.

Iittala
www.iittala.com
This website has a useful store locator and a full directory of Iittala's glassware products.

Ikea
Stores worldwide
www.ikea.com
The PS and Air collections are always worth a look for slightly more cutting-edge designs from this Swedish giant.

Inhouse
28 Howe Street
Edinburgh EH3 6TG
+44 (0)131 225 2888
www.inhouse-uk.com
Mainly accessories, with goods from Iittala and Stelton.

Jieldé
www.voltexdesign.com
These French anglepoise lamps suit the simple Scandinavian look.

Klassik Moderne Møbelkunst
www.klassik.dk
This shop stocks contemporary furniture and lighting by leading Scandinavian designers such as Kaare Klint and Poul Henningsen. Worldwide shipping available.

Ole Lynggaard Copenhagen
www.olelynggaard.com
Beautiful handcrafted jewellery.

Marimekko
www.marimekko.com
Bags, clothing, fabrics, kitchen, bedroom and bathroom accessories.

Moroso
www.moroso.it
This Italian design company produces furnishing that complement the Scandinavian look perfectly.

Orrefors
www.orrefors.us
Online shop for Orrefors Swedish glassware, including pieces designed by Ingegerd Råman.

Planet Bazaar
Arch 68, The Stables Market
Chalk Farm Road
London NW1 8AH
+44 (0)20 7485 6000
www.planetbazaar.co.uk
Some Danish glass and furniture.

SCP
135–139 Curtain Road
London EC2A 3BX
+44 (0)20 7739 1869
www.scp.co.uk
Besides selling British and Italian designs, SCP stocks Alvar Aalto and Arne Jacobsen furniture together with Poul Henningsen. Also some Scandinavian accessories.

Shannon
68 Walcot Street
Bath BA1 5BD
+44 (0)1225 424222
www.shannon-uk.com
This shop has a good selection of Marimekko, Iittala and furniture by designers such as Hans Wegner.

Sigmar
263 King's Road
London SW3 5EL
www.sigmarlondon.com
Scandi-style with a retro twist, curated by the stylish owners who also undertake interior design jobs.

Skandium
86 Marylebone High Street
London W1U 4QS
plus other branches
+44 (0)20 7584 2066
www.skandium.com
The single largest retailer of original Scandinavian design in the UK. Designers include Woodnotes and Arabia. Furniture, lighting, textiles, glassware, crockery, cutlery, books and gifts from manufacturers in Denmark, Finland, Norway and Sweden. Design classics and exciting modern designs.

Stelton
www.stelton.com
Showcases leading designers in Scandinavia, past and present

Svenskt Tenn
www.svenksttenn.se
Josef Frank's vibrant textiles are available, together with other goodies from this classic Stockholm store.

Scandi Living
www.scandiliving.com
UK online stockist of some of Scandinavia's leading brands.

Swedish Interior Design
+44 (0)7958 788555
www.swedishinteriordesign.co.uk
Emporium of antiques, specializing in the Gustavian period – they even sell sofas made from old sleighs!

Tangram
33/37 Jeffrey Street
Edinburgh EH1 1DH
+44 (0)131 556 6551
www.tangramfurnishers.co.uk
Mainly a contract showroom but equally welcoming to the public. The Scandinavian products on offer include Lammhults furniture, along with Woodnotes rugs and blinds.

Twentytwentyone
274 Upper Street
London N1 2UA
+44 (0)20 7288 1996
www.twentytwentyone.com
Good selection of both new and vintage furniture and accessories, including pieces by David Design.

Vitra
www.vitra.com
Manufacturer of several classic Verner Panton designs that are now back in production, as well as accessories by Charles and Ray Eames.

Vola
www.vola.com
Quality taps and bathroom fittings from this Danish retailer. Showrooms across the UK.

Woodnotes
www.woodnotes.fi
Specializing in wood fibre rugs, floor cushions, seating cubes and other accessories. Locate your nearest retailer on the website.

case study credits

Caroline Clifton-Mogg
family friendly
eclectic harmony

Jo Denbury
northern lights

Magnus Englund & Chrystina Schmidt
understated comfort
norwegian wood
modern natural
genius in glass
cabin fever
moving lodge
rural retreat
house on stilts
designer home
among the trees

Sara Norrman
natural charm
simple style
swedish vintage
salvaging the past
worldly surrounds
antique & modern
raw luxury

picture credits

page 11 ph Debi Treloar/owner of Crème de la Crème à la Edgar, Helle Høgsbro Krag's home in Copenhagen; 1cl ph Paul Ryan/the summerhouse of Peter Morgan at the Bjäte peninsula; 1cr ph Winfried Heinze/the apartment of Lars Kristensen owner of Fil de Fer, Copenhagen; 1r ph Andrew Wood/Antti Nurmesniemi's house in Helsinki, Finland; 2 ph Lisa Cohen/the designer Nina Hartmann's home in Sweden, www.vintagebynina.com; 3 ph Debi Treloar/designer Susanne Rutzou's home in Copenhagen; 4 ph Andrew Wood/Ristomatti Ratia's apartment in Helsinki, Finland; 5 ph Debi Treloar/designer Susanne Rutzou's home in Copenhagen; 6 ph Debi Treloar/Cristine Tholstrup Hermansen and Helge Drenck's house in Copenhagen; 7 ph Debi Treloar/ceramicist Jette Arendal Winther's home in Denmark, www.arendal-ceramics.com; 8 ph Debi Treloar/Christina & Allan Thaulow's home in Denmark; 9 ph Debi Treloar/ Sanne Hjermind and Claes Bech-Poulsen; 10 ph Andrew Wood/Christer Wallensteen's apartment in Stockholm, Sweden; 11 ph Paul Ryan/the summerhouse of Mikko Pulkkinen in Kustovi, Finland (built in 1967); 12 ph Andrew Wood/Into Tasa's house in Espoo, Finland, designed by architect Jyrki Tasa; 14–21 ph Paul Ryan; 22–27 ph Winfried Heinze/the home of Kamilla Bryiel and Christian Permin in Copenhagen; 28–37 ph Paul Massey/the home in Denmark of Charlotte Lynggaard, designer of Ole Lynggaard Copenhagen; 38–43 ph Chris Tubbs; 44–51 ph Paul Massey/kitchen by Rasmus Larsson, Design By Us; 52–57 ph Winfried Heinze/the apartment of Lars Kristensen owner of Fil de Fer, Copenhagen; 58 ph Debi Treloar/ceramicist Jette Arendal Winther's home in Denmark, www.arendal-ceramics.com; 60–67 ph Lisa Cohen/ the designer Nina Hartmann's home in Sweden, www.vintagebynina.com; 68–75 ph Debi Treloar/Martin Nannestad Jørgensen; 76–83 ph Lisa Cohen/ the home of Lars Wiberg of Pour Quoi in Copenhagen; 84–91 ph Polly Wreford/Indenfor & Udenfor in Copenhagen (home and shop near the royal castle); 92 ph Andrew Wood/Ristomatti Ratia's apartment in Helsinki, Finland; 94–99 ph Paul Ryan/a house designed by Ilkka Suppanen in Finland; 100–105 ph Paul Ryan/the home of Ingegerd Raman and Claes Söderquist's home in Sweden; 106–113 ph Paul Massey/Naja Lauf; 114–117 ph Andrew Wood/ Mikko Puotila's apartment in Espoo, Finland, interior design by Ulla Koskinen; 118 ph Andrew Wood/architect Grethe Meyer's house, Hørsholm, Denmark; 120–125 ph Paul Ryan/summer house at Hvasser, of Astir Eidsbo and Tore Lindholm; 126–129 ph Paul Ryan/the summer home of Elina Helenius and Mika Mahlberg in Finland; 130–135 ph Paul Ryan/the home of Nils Tunebjer in Sweden; 136–143 ph Paul Ryan/Aki Wahlman's summer home in Finland; 144–147 ph Andrew Wood/Matti and Pirjo Sanaksenaho's house in Espoo, designed by Matti and Pirjo Sanaksenaho, Sanaksenaho Architects; 148–153 ph Paul Ryan; 155 & 157 ph Paul Ryan/Ritva Puotila's summerhome in Finland.

KEY: ph= photographer, r=right, l=left, c=centre

business credits

Antti Nurmesniemi
Architect, designer professor
Studio Nurmesniemi / Antti
Nurmesniemi
+358 9 684 7055
fax: +358 9 684 8325
Page 1 right

Arkkitehdit NRT Oy
Nurmela-Raimorantia-Tasa
Kalevankatu 31
00100 Helsinki
Finland
+358 9 6866780
tasa@n-r-t.fi
www.n-r-t.fi
Page 12

Claes Bech-Poulsen
Photographer
+45 40 19 93 99
claes@claesbp.com
www.claesbp.dk
Page 9

Claesson Koivisto Rune
Arkitektkontor
Sankt Paulsgatan 25
SE-118 48 Stockholm
Sweden
+46 8 644 5863
arkitektkontor@claesson-kovisto-rune.se
Pages 100–105

Crème de la Crème à la Edgar
Kompagnistræde 8,st
1208 Copenhagen K
+45 33361818
www.cremedelacremealaedgar.dk
Page 1 left

Design By Us
www.design-by-us.com
also summer house in South of
France
available to rent:
www.villalagachon.com
Pages 44–51

Fil de Fer
Store Kongensgade 83 A
1264 Copenhagen K
Denmark
+45 33 32 32 46
fildefer@fildefer.dk
www.fildefer.dk
Pages 1 centre right, 52–57

Gert Wingardh – architect
Wingårdhs
Kungsgatan 10A
SE411 19 Göteborg
Sweden
+46 31 743 7000
Page 1 centre left

Grethe Meyer
Designer and architect MAA
Royal Scandinavia A/S
Smallegade 45
2000 Frederiksberg
Denmark
+45 38 14 48 48
Page 118

Ilkka Suppanen
Studio Suppanen
Sturenkatu 13
00510 Helsinki
Finland
+35 8 9 622 78737
fax: +35 8 9 622 3093
info@suppanen.com
www.suppanen.com
Pages 94–99

Indenfor & Udenfor
Toldbodgade 65 b
1253 Copenhagen K
Denmark
+45 22 34 94 53
info@indenfor.com
www.indenfor.com
Pages 84–91

Ingegerd Raman
Bergsgafan 53
SE-11231 Stockholm
Sweden
+46 8 6502824
ingegerd.raman@orrefors.se
Pages 100–105

Jette Arendal Winther
www.arendal-ceramics.com
Pages 7, 58

Lund & Hagem Arkitektur AS
Filipstadun 5,
0250 Oslo
Norway
+47 23 33 31 50
mail@lundhagem.no
www.lundhagem.no
Pages 120–125

Martin Nannestad Jørgensen
www.martinnannestad.dk
Pages 68–75

Mikko Pulkkinen
Architect M.Sc, SAFA
Finland
Mikko.pulkkinen@ark-lpr.fi
Page 11

Naja Lauf A/S
Strandvejen 340,
DK-2930 Klampenborg
+45 7025 1325
nl@najalauf.dk
www.najalauf.dk
Pages 106–113

Nina Hartmann
www.vintagebynina.com
Pages 2, 60–67

Ole Lynggaard Copenhagen
Hellerupvej 15B
DK - 2900 Hellerup
+45 39 46 03 00
www.olelynggaard.com
Pages 28–37

Peter Hulting, architect
Meter Arkitektur
Kolonigatan 4
413 21 Göteborg
Sweden
+46 31 204330
peter@meterarkitektur.se
www.meterarkitektur.se
Pages 148–153

Pour Quoi
Nodre Frihavnsgade 13
2100 Copenhagen
Denmark
+45 35 26 62 54
Pages 76–83

Ratia Brand Co Oy
Kapteeninkatu 1 E
00140 Helsinki
Finland
+358 9 622 72820
ratia@ratia.com
www.ratia.com
Pages 4, 92

Rützou A/S
+45 35240616
cph@rutzou.com
www.rutzou.com
Pages 3, 5

Sanaksenaho Architects
Tehtaankatu 27-29D
00150 Helsinki
Finland
+358 9 177 341
ark@sanaksenaho.com
www.kolumbus.fi/sanaksenaho
Pages 126–129, 143–147

Sanne Hjermind
Artist
+45 26 91 01 97
Page 9

Stella Nova ApS
Hauser Plads 32, 1st Floor
DK-1128 Copenahgen K
Denmark
+45 33 30 89 89
info@stella-nova.dk
www.stella-nova.dk
pages 22–27

Stenhuset Antikhandel
Bögerups gård
24196 Stockamöllan
Sweden
+46 70 965 9565
www.stenhusetantikhandel.com
Pages 38–43

Studio Elina Helenius
Orioninkatu 10–12,
00550 Helsinki
Finland
mail@elinahelenius.com
www.elinahelenius.com
Pages 126–129

Tore Lindholm
tore.lindholm@nchr.uio.no
Pages 120–125

Wallensteen & Co aab
Architect and Design Consultants
Floragatan 11
114 31 Stockholm
Sweden
+46 8 210151
wallensteen@chello.se
Lighting: Konkret Architects/Gerhard
Rehm
Page 10

Woodnotes OY
Tallberginkatu 1B
00180 Helsinki
Finland
+358 9694 2200
woodnotes@woodnotes.fi
www.woodnotes.fi
Pages 114–117, 155, 157

index

Figures in *italics* indicate photographs.